WHO READS LITERATURE?

WHO READS LITERATURE?

The Future of the United States as a Nation of Readers

Nicholas Zill
and
Marianne Winglee

Foreword by
Jonathan Yardley

SEVEN LOCKS PRESS
Cabin John, Md / Washington, DC

Who Reads Literature? is Report #22 in a series on matters of interest to the arts community commissioned by the Research Division of the National Endowment for the Arts.

Foreword © by *The Washington Post.* It originally appeared in *The Washington Post* on August 28, 1989. It is reprinted here with permission of the author and *The Washington Post.*

Library of Congress Cataloging-in-Publication Data

Zill, Nicholas.
    Who reads literature? : the future of the United States as a nation of readers / Nicholas Zill and Marianne Winglee : foreword by Jonathan Yardley.
       p. cm. — (Research Division report / National Endowment for the Arts ; 22)
       ISBN 0-932020-86-0 : $9.95
       1. Books and reading—United States—Forecasting. 2. Literature—Appreciation—United States—Forecasting. I. Winglee, Marianne. II. Title. III. Series: Research Division report (National Endowment for the Arts. Research Division) : 22.
Z1003.2.Z54   1990   90-33699
028'.9'093—dc20   CIP

Manufactured in the United States of America
Designed by Giles Bayley
Cover design by Betsy Bayley
Typeset by Bets, LTD, Ithaca, NY
Printed by McNaughton & Gunn, Saline, MI

Seven Locks Press is a Washington-based book publisher of nonfiction works on social, political and cultural issues. It takes its name from a series of lift locks on the Chesapeake and Ohio Canal.

For more information or a catalog:

Seven Locks Press
P.O. Box 27
Cabin John, MD 20818
(301) 320-2130

Contents

Foreword

Several years ago Walker Percy wondered aloud, in the pages of a national magazine, about the number of Americans who actually buy, read, and discuss serious contemporary literature. It was, he thought, a pathetically small number, perhaps one percent of the adult population or even less: a serious literary community, that is, of somewhere between one and two million Americans, scarcely a consequential quantity in a culture where audiences in the tens of millions are routinely tuned into television sitcoms and sporting events.

This gloomy assessment caused a flurry of controversy among the lit'ry folk; they had assumed themselves to be a far larger crowd, if not indeed a horde, so not merely to be disabused of this notion but to have the message brought by one of their own was anything except pleasant. But the stir came and went quickly, in the main because no one had any hard evidence to refute Percy's complaint and also because, let's face it, not many outside the literary community were interested.

Still, the questions won't go away: Who reads serious literature in the United States, and how many of them are there? These are matters of continuing interest to authors, scholars, and others whose careers are predicated on the existence of a viable literary community, and they are of interest as well to those whose investment is more overtly commercial: publishers, booksellers and wholesalers, journalists, and other media folk. Like any other group in our economy, the literary community is a market to be identified and exploited by those with something to sell to it; thus its size and character are matters of more than passing interest to some persons and institutions that are not, themselves, necessarily members of it.

In these circumstances it is useful to have a *Who Reads Literature: The Future of the United States as a Nation of Readers.* As one can quickly surmise, it is the work of people who specialize in the jargon of the social sciences: Nicholas Zill, a social psychologist, and Marianne Winglee, a statistical analyst. They have assembled a good deal of valuable information and they have managed to make a degree of sense out of it.

As so often happens when the voodoo priests of sociology, psychology and statistics work their solemn magic on human behavior, what this survey does is tell us, in statistics and analysis, what we know already through empirical observation: that Walker Percy was right. Zill and Winglee have their hearts in the right place and earnestly wish the evidence told them otherwise, but what their numbers add up to is that (a) "the proportion [of Americans] who read serious literature of all forms in the course of a year seems to be about 7 to 12 percent of the adult population" and that (b) "literature reading" is "stagnant or even declining, when various demographic factors indicate that it should be increasing."

Even that figure of 7 to 12 percent is shaky at best, for people who claim to be regular readers often admit, when pressed for specifics, that they are regular readers not of Saul Bellow and Eudora Welty but of Stephen King and Danielle Steele; if we restrict readers of literature to "those familliar with excellent but not widely known authors, such as poets Adrienne Rich or James Merrill, then the size of the audience for contemporary literature would become minuscule indeed." Not merely that but—as anyone keeping a close eye on literary matters should realize—to a striking degree this readership is defined by sex, education and income:

> ...if we had to put together a picture of a typical reader of literature in the United States today, the survey data indicate that the person would be a middle-aged white female living in the suburbs of a Western or Midwestern city. She would have a college education, and a middle- to upper-middle class income that was not derived from her literary activities. She would be an active and involved individual, not a passive or reclusive one. She would not only read books and magazines, and occasionally try her hand at poetry or fiction, but also participate in a variety of indoor, outdoor and community activities.

And authors wonder why they're sent to book-and-author luncheons in Cleveland and Minneapolis! The explanation is simple: That's where the readers are—not merely the readers of Judith Krantz and Belva Plain, but also the readers of Laurie Colwin and Gloria Naylor. The perceived image of the "literary" American reader as a bearded male academic in a tweed jacket with leather patches bears only scant connection to reality; the reader who really supports serious American literature, such of it as there still may be, is far more likely to be an educated woman of a certain age who belongs to a neighborhood book club, buys her clothes through the mail from Talbots, contributes to Greenpeace, and does volunteer work at the House of Ruth.

Though Zill and Winglee do not say so, there is a reason to believe that this has been so for a couple of generations. But now literature is beginning to catch up with its readers. "It can be argued," Zill and Winglee claim, "that the kinds of works being published by literary presses in the United States today are very much a reflection of the interests and concerns of this typical reader," and they are absolutely right.

If a single generalization can be made about contemporary American literature, apart from its roots in the creative-writing schools, it would be that it is the province of middle- and upper-middle-class women. If in the past they were the readers, now they are the writers as well. The point has been made before, but it is worth making again: While male writers of serious literature under the age of 40 are notable in the United States largely for their absence or their lack of consequence, female writers of their generation are notable both for their numbers and for the quality of their work. Unquestionably, Zill and Winglee are right:

> The women's movement may be stimulating female involvement with literature. Whenever norms and values are in flux, literature has a special role to play. Literature can explore new patterns of behavior, provide characters that serve as role models, and give voice to both the exhilaration and the frustrations that pioneers experience. The drive for women's rights has helped to draw attention to outstanding women writers of the past and present, and to open more opportunities for women in the publishing and promotion of literature.

How large those opportunities will be is questionable at best: The world of American literature is small by any standard, and over the long haul is most unlikely to grow larger, in real if not numerical terms. But it's a woman's world now, and if we are to have in the next generation a literature of any consequence, it will be because women make it so.

Jonathan Yardley

This article originally appeared in The Washington Post *on August 28, 1989. It is reprinted with the permission of the author and* The Washington Post.

Introduction

Because the art of literature is inextricably linked to a country's language and history, it has traditionally played a central role in the culture of most nations. It is difficult to think of England without thinking of Shakespeare and Dickens, or Russia without Pushkin, Tolstoy, Chekhov, and Dostoyevsky. So it has been in the United States, at least in the past. The American cultural heritage includes characters, scenes, and phrases from the works of such authors as Washington Irving, Edgar Allan Poe, Henry David Thoreau, Herman Melville, Walt Whitman, Emily Dickinson, Mark Twain, Ernest Hemingway, and Eugene O'Neill, among others.

Today, however, there is a widespread sense that the reading of literature does not occupy a prominent place in the lives of most Americans. Many observers feel that we are no longer "a nation of readers," but a nation of watchers: watchers of movies, television, videocassettes, and computer displays. Literary critic and newspaper columnist Jonathan Yardley complains about the "increasing irrelevance of writing," and laments the fact that contemporary American poets, from the laureate on down, are all but un-known to the American people.[1] University of Chicago professor Allan Bloom, author of *The Closing of the American Mind,* asserts that "our students have lost the practice of and taste for reading. They have not learned how to read, nor do they have the expectation of delight or improvement from reading."[2] University of Virginia professor E. D. Hirsch sounds a similar theme in his book *Cultural Literacy,* contending that writers and speakers can no longer take it for granted that young readers and listeners will be familiar with works, characters, and authors that used to be known by all educated people.[3] There is even a new term, "aliteracy," that has been coined to describe the phenomenon of people who know how to read but choose not to do so.[4]

There is empirical evidence that seems to support these contentions. For example, one national study found that U.S. adults spend four times as much leisure time watching television or listening to the radio as they do reading books, magazines, or newspapers.[5] There are also survey results showing the American public to be ignorant about basic literary matters. A 1984 University of Maryland survey found that only one quarter of American adults knew who George Orwell, the celebrated author of the novel *1984,* was.[6] In 1986, the Educational Testing Service conducted a national assessment of the literary and historical knowledge of high school juniors. The Service found that less than 30 percent of them could identify Tennessee Williams as the author of *A Streetcar Named Desire,* and less than a quarter knew something about the plot of *A Catcher in the Rye.*[7] Indeed, it seems possible that students in the Soviet Union, who are known to be avid readers of American literature, would do better at recognizing the works of these and other modern American writers than students in the United States.

Other evidence indicates, however, that for both reading in general and literature reading in particular the situation may not be quite so bleak. To begin with, there are a lot of books sold in the United States: more than two billion each year during the mid-1980s, or about nine books for every person over five years of age. About 500 million of these are relatively inexpensive, "mass market" paperbacks.[8] Many of the paperbacks contain works of fiction, even if most of the titles might not qualify as what literary critics would call literature.

Furthermore, the Educational Testing Service's assessment found that virtually all high school students received some training in the appreciation of literature and are made to read at least a few classic works by English and American authors. As a consequence, today's students are still likely to know something about Shakespeare, Dickens, Hawthorne, and F. Scott Fitzgerald.[9] By contrast, relatively few receive formal training in the visual arts, music, or dance, and usually have only the foggiest of notions about Jackson Pollock, George Gershwin, Charlie Parker, or Martha Graham.[10]

But do young people go on to read literature when they leave school and are no longer required to do so? Of all the arts, literature should be the one with the widest following. Only a minority of young people learn to read music or play an instrument, draw or paint proficiently, or act or dance on stage. But everyone who is educable is expected to learn to read and write.[11]

Assessing the State of Literature Reading

We can infer from bestseller lists that American adults read real estate investment guides, personal computer manuals, diet cookbooks, and the like. Do they also read novels, poetry, and plays? The number of works of fiction published in the U.S. each year—about 5,100 new titles or new editions[12]—suggests that some people still read novels and short stories. This inference is reinforced by the large number of fiction books sold each year—some 400 million copies through general retail outlets alone.[13] To be sure, many of the fiction titles published and sold are works of genre fiction—thrillers, romances, science fiction, and the like—most of which would not be considered works of high literature. Nevertheless, even among the genre titles there are works written with considerable craft and imagination, and read with enthusiasm by people who could be spending their time watching movies or television. In addition to the large output of fiction, there are about 1,000 volumes of poetry and drama published each year, and nearly 2,000 books of literary criticism and literary commentary.[14]

Clearly, the writing and reading of literature are not yet defunct.

But we need more than publication and sales figures to form an accurate picture of how much literature reading is going on in the United States. A person can buy a book without ever getting around to reading it, or read a book that has not been bought, but borrowed from a friend or a library. And literature is published in periodicals as well as books. Thus we need information about the reading habits of representative samples of American citizens, including specifics about the kinds of books they read. Several large surveys on participation in the arts or on book reading were carried out in the United States during the 1980s for exactly this purpose.

One of the most notable of these is the Survey of Public Participation in the Arts (SPPA), which was a nationwide survey, designed and sponsored by the National Endowment for the Arts and conducted in 1982 and 1985 by the U.S. Bureau of the Census. Issues not covered in the SPPA are examined in data drawn from book industry publication and sales statistics, and from two other national surveys: the Arts-Related Trend Study (ARTS) carried out in 1983-1984 by the Survey Research Center at the University of Maryland, and the Consumer Research Study on Reading and Book Purchasing done in 1983 for the Book Industry Study Group (BISG).[15]

There are, of course, problems in using survey data to study literature reading. Some of these problems are common to all surveys that ask people to report on their own behavior, while others are unique to studies of reading. British sociologist Peter Mann points out that there are problems associated with research into reading "which arise from the difficulty in determining what is meant by 'reading' and what constitutes a 'book'."[16] Research on the reading of literature is even more problematic because of disagreements among experts on what should be included under the rubric of "literature" and the difficulty of framing general and easily understood questions about such reading.

Here, the reading of literature or what we will simply call "reading" means the reading of novels, short stories, poetry, and plays. As usually defined, literature also subsumes such high-quality, non-fiction writing as essays, literary criticism, literary commentary, "belles lettres," biographies, and the so-called "non-fiction novel." However, these forms of literature were not explicitly covered in the surveys discussed here. In addition, distinctions between art and entertainment, based on the quality or seriousness of the written work, are very important. Unfortunately, most of these surveys do not include information that permits one to say something about the quality of the books and magazine pieces that American adults are reading. This kind of information was collected in two of the other surveys described, but, even with these data, drawing the line between literature and mere amusement is no simple matter.

Because of the great expense and practical difficulties involved in trying to observe directly the reading habits of large numbers of Americans, the survey results presented here rely on people's reports about the kinds of works they have read or not read within broad intervals of time (the last 12 months or the last 6 months). These reports are subject to both systematic bias and random error. To the extent that reading literature is perceived as something that one "ought" to be doing, people will tend to say they have read a novel or short story when, in fact, they have not. They may also "telescope" events that happened in the past, such as reading a book more than a year ago, and remember them as having occurred within the reference period in question. On the other hand, people tend to forget about things they did more than a few weeks ago, especially if the event was not very important to them, and this could result in underreporting. Accurate reporting also depends on the respondent's understanding of what is meant by terms such as "novel" and "short story," which may pose problems for less educated individuals.

Two of the surveys described here attempted to get a sense of the seriousness of some of these problems by asking respondents follow-up questions. The answers to these questions provide both further information about the works the survey respondents have read, and a basis for adjusting estimates of the size of the literature audience.

The survey situation does, however, have certain advantageous aspects that are rarely encountered in everyday life: the respondent is offered anonymity; honest reporting is explicitly encouraged;

and there is no overt praise or criticism for saying that one has or has not done something. Moreover, a survey that uses scientific sampling procedures and achieves a high response rate provides a picture of a real cross-section of the population, not just of a limited and self-selected subset of people.

Even when there is an overall bias in survey reporting on an activity, surveys can still provide an accurate reading of the comparative commonness of different forms of the activity, or of the relative frequency of the activity among different groups, or of changes in the frequency of the activity over time. It is known, for example, that people tend to overreport voting in local or national elections: there are more people who say they voted than the total number of ballots cast. Yet surveys of voting behavior still give a good sense of the relative voting rates of different age, sex, educational, ethnic, and residential groups, and show how these patterns have changed over the last several decades.

In any event, self-report surveys, with all their limitations, are the best source of information on literature reading that we have. They will remain so until government or private groups invest in studies that use direct observations of reading or ask for self-reports that cover shorter time intervals and include more people in the sample, and that elicit more extensive follow-up information on the specific titles read.

Chapter 1
Readers of Fiction, Poetry, and Drama: How Many and Who Are They?

The 1982 and 1985 rounds of the Survey of Public Participation in the Arts (SPPA) took national probability samples of adults aged 18 and over living in households in the United States. These arts surveys were done as supplements to larger survey programs involving panels of respondents who were interviewed every six months over a three-year period. In 1982, the SPPA interviewed 17,254 people, or 89 percent of the target sample. The sample was about 20 percent smaller in 1985, when 13,675 people were interviewed, or 85 percent of the target sample. Three quarters of the interviews were done in person and the remainder by telephone.[17]

The SPPA interviews focused on attendance at arts exhibitions and performances, including art museum shows, classical music concerts, opera, jazz, plays, and musicals, and on other forms of arts participation, including reading literature. In addition to a core set of questions that were asked of all respondents, subsamples were asked about training in the arts, mass media usage, and other forms of leisure activity. A basic question on the reading of novels, short stories, poetry, and plays was put to the entire sample in both surveys, but questions on other forms of literature participation and socialization were asked only of subsamples of about 4,200 to 5,500 respondents in 1982, and about 2,300 respondents in 1985.

In 1985, the SPPA found that 56 percent of a national sample of adults aged 18 and over, representing 95.2 million people, reported that they had read novels, short stories, poetry, or plays during the last 12 months. The estimated number of readers was up by nearly three million from the number in the 1982 SPPA. However, this increase was the result of population growth only. The proportion of adults who said they read literature was about the same in both years.

The 1985 survey also asked whether respondents had read *any* kind of book or magazine during the previous 12 months. Eighty-six percent—representing some 146 million adults—said that they had. If we divide the number of people who reported reading literature by the number who reported reading any kind of book or magazine, we have an estimate of literature readers as a fraction of all readers. In 1985, 65 percent of all adult readers in the U.S. read some fiction, poetry, or drama in the course of a year.[18] This was slightly lower than the 67 percent found in the 1982 survey, but the difference was within the margin of sampling error.

The SPPA collected additional information on public participation in one particular form of literature—poetry. In the 1985 survey, 19 percent of the respondents—representing 32 million adults—reported that they had read or listened to a reading of poetry during the previous 12 months. For the 1982 survey, these figures were 20 percent and 30 million, respectively. Again, the differences were not statistically significant.

In addition to questions about reading literature, the SPPA asked respondents if they had worked on "any creative writings, such as stories, poems, plays, and the like" during the last 12 months. There was no requirement that the writing had been published, and the results of an independent follow-up study indicate that most of it probably was not. In the 1985 survey, 6 percent of the respondents—representing 10.6 million adults—said that they had tried to do some creative writing. This was about the same as the 1982 results, when 7 percent—representing 10.7 million adults—

answered the question affirmatively. The apparent decline in the proportion of writers was not statistically significant.

Comparing SPPA Results with Other Surveys and Sales Figures
The levels of reading reported in the SPPA are in at least approximate agreement with the results of other nationwide surveys. For example, the Consumer Research Study on Reading and Book Purchasing conducted in 1983 for the Book Industry Study Group (BISG) found that 39 percent of all adult respondents had read a book of fiction in the last six months and half had read a book of some sort; and 92 percent had read magazines, periodicals, or newspapers over the same period.[19] Similar results have been obtained in other countries. In Britain, for instance, a number of national studies done in the late 1970s and early 1980s found that, as in the U.S., roughly half the adult population reported reading books of one sort or another. In a 1981 Euromonitor survey of about 2,000 people aged 16 and over, 45 percent said they were reading a book (any book) at the time of the survey and about 30 percent said they were reading a work of fiction.[20]

Despite the general agreement among readership studies, their estimates are typically met with incredulity by those involved with the writing, publishing, or support of contemporary literature. What literary people point out is that it is not uncommon for a work of serious fiction to sell fewer than 5,000 copies nowadays. Likewise, the circulation of most poetry magazines is counted in the low thousands or even hundreds. In 1987, the *Los Angeles Times Book Review* announced that it would no longer be reviewing new volumes of poetry because there was so little reader interest in them. Even the most widely read magazines that publish first-rate fiction and poetry—magazines like *The New Yorker* and *The Atlantic*—have circulations in only the 400,000–600,000 range.[21]

John P. Dessauer, a leading expert on book industry sales trends, has estimated that a total of 3.2 million copies of contemporary literary fiction and poetry books were sold through general retailers in 1985, representing just 0.3 percent of all books sold through these outlets. Sales of classic works of literature made up another 9.1 million units, or 0.9 percent of books sold. Thus, contemporary and classic literature together constituted little more than one percent of bookstore sales.[22] If there are so many readers of literature out there, why do the literary books and magazines not sell better?

Of course, people get reading material from friends and relatives, from public libraries, in doctors' and dentists' offices, and from their own stock of books acquired over the years. When fiction readers surveyed in the BISG study were asked where they had obtained the last book they had read, less than half—45 percent—said they had purchased it themselves. More than a quarter said they borrowed the book from a friend or relative or traded it for another book. Another fifth had borrowed the book from a library, and 5 percent had received it as a gift.[23] However, even doubling or tripling the estimated number of literature books sold to account for books borrowed and exchanged would not bring the total close to the 95 million readers that the SPPA found.

What *does* bring the survey and book sales figures into line with one another is incorporating the large numbers of copies of romances, thrillers, science fiction novels, and other works of popular or genre fiction that are sold each year. John Dessauer estimates that total sales of "popular fiction" books through general retail outlets amounted to more than 322 million copies in 1985. And that does not include nearly 124 million in "bestseller" sales. (Assuming that about two-thirds of the bestsellers were fiction would bring the total number of popular fiction books sold through general retail outlets to about 400 million.)[24]

Thus, what most of the survey respondents seem to be talking about when they report that they have read novels or short stories are works of relatively light, genre fiction. Inasmuch as many of these works would not qualify as literature in the eyes of most literary critics, the implication is that the adult audience for serious contemporary literature is probably a good deal smaller than the 56 percent found in the SPPA. These impressions are strengthened by survey information on the specific titles or the kinds of works to which people are referring when they report that they have read fiction, poetry, or drama. Information on works read was not collected in the Survey of Public Participation in the Arts, but relevant data are available from the Arts-Related Trend Study (ARTS) conducted by the University of Maryland and the Consumer Research Study on Reading and Book Purchasing done for the Book Industry Study Group. These data are examined later.

What Kinds of People Read Literature?

Demographic Characteristics

People who report reading fiction, poetry, and drama are a diverse group. They are found in every segment of the U.S. population, except those subgroups who do not read at all. However, some segments of the population are overrepresented among readers (and writers) of literature:

- those who have at least some college education (who make up 49 percent of literature readers, as opposed to 36 percent of the general population);
- those with incomes of $25,000 and over (who comprise 48 percent of literature readers, but 40 percent of the general population);
- females (59 percent of literature readers, but 53 percent of the general population);
- the middle-aged (40 percent of literature readers, but 36 percent of the general adult population);
- whites (85 percent of literature readers, but 81 percent of the general population).

Conversely, groups that are underrepresented among literature readers include the following:

- those with less than a high-school education (who comprise 14 percent of literature readers, but 25 percent of the general population);
- those with incomes under $10,000 (16 percent of literature readers, 21 percent of the general population);
- males (41 percent of literature readers, 47 percent of the adult population);
- those aged 50 and older (32 percent of literature readers, 35 percent of the general adult population);

- Blacks and Hispanics (13 percent of literature readers, 17 percent of the general population).

As one goes from the overall population, to those who read books and magazines, to those who read literature, to those who read or listen to poetry, and to those who try to produce creative writing, the groups become progressively more college-educated, more female, and more middle-income. (Table 1.) Thus, of the self-described writers in the 1985 SPPA, 69 percent were college-educated, 63 percent were female, and 51 percent had incomes of $25,000 or more. (Given that most of the writing reported in the SPPA was probably unpublished, and that even when published, writing is usually not handsomely rewarded, we can be confident that the income of these creative writers came primarily from sources other than their writings.)

The relationships between literary participation and personal characteristics, such as education, income, age, sex, and race, as well as the reasons behind the observed relationships, are examined in greater detail later.

Geographic Distribution

The writing, publishing, and reading of literature are often thought of as Northeastern, big-city enterprises. But the arts survey data show that these readers and writers are spread throughout the four major regions of the country, pretty much in line with the distribution of the total adult population. (Table 1.) If any region was overrepresented, it was the West. In 1985, for example, the West contained 19 percent of the overall adult population, but had 22 percent of the readers and 33 percent of the writers of literature. The Midwest, with 25 percent of the adult population, had 26 percent of readers and 30 percent of writers. The South tended to be underrepresented in this regard. But, being the largest region in terms of overall population, the South contained nearly a third of all readers and almost a quarter of all writers.

The majority of readers and writers do live in the large metropolitan areas of the country. But, like the rest of the more educated and affluent population, most of them live in the suburbs, not the central cities. In 1985, the suburbs held 41 percent of the

TABLE I. Size and Composition of U.S. Population of Adult Readers and Writers of Literature, by Age, Gender, Ethnic Group, Education, Income, Region, and Metropolitan Residence, U.S. Adults Aged 18 and Over, 1985.

	Total Adult Population	All Readers	Literature Readers	Poetry Readers	Creative Literature Writers
No. in population (in millions)	170.6	146.0	95.2	31.8	10.6
% of Adult Pop.	100%	86%	56%	19%	6%
% of All Readers	—	100%	65%	22%	7%
TOTAL	100%	100%	100%	100%	100%
			Percent Distribution		
AGE					
Young (18-29)	28%	29%	29%	30%	39%
Middle (30-49)	36%	38%	40%	38%	44%
Older (50 +)	35%	33%	32%	32%	17%
GENDER					
Female	53%	54%	59%	60%	63%
Male	47%	46%	41%	40%	37%
ETHNIC GROUP					
White	81%	85%	85%	86%	87%
Black	11%	8%	8%	8%	8%
Hispanic	7%	5%	5%	5%	4%
Asian, Other	2%	2%	2%	2%	1%
EDUCATION					
Some College	36%	42%	49%	56%	69%
High School Grad	39%	38%	37%	30%	23%
Less than HS	25%	20%	14%	15%	8%
INCOME					
$25K & over	40%	45%	48%	47%	51%
$10-25K	39%	38%	36%	39%	39%
Under $10K	21%	17%	16%	15%	10%
REGION					
Northeast	21%	19%	21%	17%	13%
Midwest	25%	27%	26%	32%	30%
South	34%	32%	31%	33%	24%
West	19%	23%	22%	19%	33%
RESIDENCE					
Central City	27%	25%	27%	26%	32%
Suburbs	41%	45%	45%	45%	53%
Non-Metro	32%	30%	28%	29%	15%

SOURCE: National Endowment for the Arts and U.S. Bureau of the Census, 1985 Survey of Public Participation in the Arts, tabulations by N. Zill and M. Winglee from public use data files.

general adult population, but 45 percent of the readers and 53 percent of the writers. The comparable figures for the central cities, with 27 percent of the population, are 27 and 32 percent, respectively. People living outside of metropolitan areas were under-represented: these areas contained 32 percent of the adult population in 1985, but only 28 percent of the literature readers and just 15 percent of the writers.

Leisure Activity Profile

In the report on the 1983 Book Industry Study Group (BISG) survey of book reading habits, the following note was made:

> Book readers are often portrayed in literature, films, or on stage as solitary, somewhat aloof, self-absorbed personalities whose devotion to their books seems to take the place of interaction with the rest of the world. This study, however, proves the stereotype to be nothing more than a myth. Far from being introverted or social outcasts, book readers emerge as well-rounded individuals active in a wide range of social and cultural activities.[25]

The BISG study found that book readers were more active than non-book readers in many areas, including that of socializing with others.

The SPPA obtained a very similar result. In addition to information about literature reading and arts attendance, the SPPA collected data on participation in a variety of other leisure activities during the 12 months prior to the survey. When the reports on recreational activities were cross-tabulated with the measures of literary participation, it was found that people who had read fiction, poetry, and drama in the last year were more active in virtually all areas than people who had done reading, but not of literature. The latter group was more active, in turn, than those who had not read any books or magazines at all. (Table 2.)

Literature readers were not only more active in areas where one might expect them to be (e.g., visiting arts fairs, historic sites, and museums; doing gardening or gourmet cooking; or taking part in arts and crafts activities), they were also more active in going to less refined amusement events: playing games and sports; tak-

TABLE 2. Leisure Activity Profile of Total Adult Population, Literature Readers, Non-Literature Readers, and Non-Readers, U.S. Adults Aged 18 and Over, 1982.

LEISURE ACTIVITIES	Total Adult Population	Literature Readers	Readers, But Not of Literature	Non-Readers
	READERSHIP GROUPS			
	Proportion of Group That Has Done Activity in Last 12 Months			
Amusements				
Play card, board games	65%	77%	62%	27%
Attend movies	63%	75%	59%	25%
Visit amusement park	49%	57%	49%	19%
Attend sports events	48%	59%	43%	17%
Exercise, Sports				
Jog, exercise	52%	65%	43%	18%
Play sports	39%	48%	36%	14%
Camping, hiking	37%	43%	34%	14%
Home-Based Activities				
Repair home, car	60%	66%	60%	28%
Gardening	61%	69%	53%	34%
Gourmet cooking	29%	38%	22%	8%
Collect stamps, coins	15%	20%	10%	3%
Charitable Activities				
Volunteer, charity work	28%	36%	21%	9%
Cultural Attendance				
Visit art/crafts fairs	39%	54%	28%	10%
Visit historic sites	37%	50%	28%	8%
Go to zoo	32%	41%	25%	11%
Visit science, natural history museums	23%	32%	15%	4%
Art & Crafts Activities				
Weaving, needlework	33%	42%	29%	18%
Pottery, ceramics	13%	17%	9%	3%
Photography, video	10%	14%	6%	2%
Painting, drawing, sculpture, printmaking	10%	14%	6%	2%
Backstage theatre help	3%	4%	1%	0%
READERSHIP GROUP SIZE				
% of Adult Population	100%	57%	26%	15%

SOURCE: National Endowment for the Arts and U.S. Bureau of the Census, 1982 Survey of Public Participation in the Arts, tabulations by N. Zill and M. Winglee from public use data files.

ing part in outdoor activities; doing home and car repairs; and contributing their time to charity. For example, three quarters of the literature readers had gone to the movies in the last year, whereas less than 60 percent of the non-literature readers and only a quarter of the non-readers had done so. Two thirds of the literature readers had done jogging or other similar exercise, whereas less than half of the non-literature readers, and less than a fifth of the non-readers, had participated in some form of exercise program. More than a third of the literature readers had done volunteer or charity work, compared with a fifth of the non-literature readers and a tenth of the non-readers.

The higher activity levels of the literature readers were partly a function of their being better educated, more affluent, and younger, on the average, than their counterparts. There may also have been an element of shared reporting bias in the associations, in the sense that respondents who were more likely to remember and report one kind of activity were more apt to remember and report other kinds as well. Nonetheless, there does seem to be a genuine link between literature reading and other cultural and recreational activities.

It is not that reading literature caused the other activities, or vice versa. Rather, individuals seem to differ in their overall curiosity and activity levels, and those who have the interests and energy to do one kind of cultural or recreational activity are more likely to do others also. In some cases, there is a common thread linking literature reading with other activities, as when an individual has an interest in the Civil War, and reads historical novels about that period, visits Civil War battle sites, and goes to military museums. Even lacking a common interest, however, the operative principle seems to be the more, the more, rather than one activity versus the other.[26]

Thumbnail Sketch of the Literature Reader
In sum, if we had to put together a picture of a typical reader of literature in the United States today, the survey data indicate that the person would be a middle-aged white female living in the suburbs of a Western or Midwestern city. She would have a college education, and a middle- to upper-middle class income that

was not derived from her literary activities. She would be an active and involved individual, not a passive or reclusive one. She would not only read books and magazines, and occasionally try her hand at poetry or fiction, but also participate in a variety of indoor, outdoor, and community activities.

Obviously, there are many readers and creative writers who do not conform to this stereotype. Indeed, one of the heartening aspects of the contemporary literary scene is its ethnic and cultural diversity. Nonetheless, it can be argued that the kinds of works that are being published by literary presses in the U.S. today are very much a reflection of the interests and concerns of this typical reader.

Is Literature Reading Growing or Diminishing?

There are a number of reasons for believing that the audience for literature should be growing. As the U.S. population gradually changes, older cohorts are being replaced by those whose parents had more education and were more apt to have encouraged their children to read. The younger cohorts have also had more years of schooling and are more likely to have been exposed to creative writing courses. As shown later, all of these factors are positively associated with literature reading as an adult. Thus, while we could expect that there should be more literature reading occurring in the future, it is not clear that this growth will really take place. Taken together, the 1982 and 1985 rounds of the SPPA indicate that the proportion of literature readers is holding steady, while the number of readers is growing with the overall population. However, because the two rounds of the survey are separated by just three years, we can glean only a limited picture of the longer-range changes that may be taking place. It should be possible to get a clearer view of long-term trends by viewing the SPPA findings in conjunction with the results of other surveys and book sales data from the publishing industry.

Book Reading: Past Growth, Recent Decline

It does seem to be the case that a greater proportion of the public reads books now than did so several decades ago. Data from

Gallup polls conducted in 1955 and 1984 show a 50 percent increase over that period in the proportion of respondents who reported that they had read a book (other than the Bible) "yesterday." The proportion grew from 14 to 21 percent, with much of the increase attributable to the expansion in the portion of the population that was college educated.[27] Data from the SPPA also show that middle-aged adults do more general reading and more literature reading than older adults. (Table 3.) As demonstrated later, these differences seem to represent an historical increase in reading over successive generations rather than a decline in reading with age. But is the increase continuing? Although reading in general still seems to be growing, there is evidence to indicate that book and literature reading are not. Indeed, among young adults these forms of reading may actually be on the decline.

Evidence of a recent decline in book reading comes from two national surveys sponsored by the Book Industry Study Group (BISG). The surveys were conducted in 1978 and 1983. Whereas overall reading (including newspapers and magazines) was stable over that period, there was a 5 percentage point reduction in the proportion of adults who had read books in the previous six months. More ominously, the proportion of book readers among young adults (ages 16-20) dropped by 13 points, from 75 to 62 percent.[28]

Trends in Book Sales

Indications that literature reading represents a diminishing share of all book reading can be found in sales figures from the publishing industry. Whereas the total number of books sold each year in the U.S. grew from 1.5 billion copies in the mid-1970s to more than 2 billion in the mid-1980s, unit sales of mass market paperbacks remained fairly stationary, at about 500 million copies annually.[29] Mass-market paperbound books are, of course, the form in which much popular fiction is published or reprinted. Although sales of higher-priced "trade" paperbounds* have grown, trade books in general are capturing a decreasing share of the U.S. book market. Technical, scientific, professional, and reference works are

---

*As used here, the term "trade books" includes fiction and general-interest nonfiction in hard cover and higher-priced paperbound editions, juvenile books, and mass market paperbacks.

capturing an increasing share of the market. While total annual book sales in the U.S. grew from $2.3 billion in 1968 to a projected $12.8 billion in 1988, the trade book segment of the market declined from 30 to 23 percent over the same period.[30]

Declining Reading by Young Adults

Figures from the two SPPA studies indicated constancy, rather than decreases, in the overall proportion of literature readers in the population. (Table 3.) Their data suggested declines in poetry and writing, but the observed changes may be due to sampling fluctuations. Among those under 30, however, there were statistically significant changes between the two surveys: literature reading dropped from 61 to 57 percent; poetry reading fell from 24 to 20 percent; and overall reading declined from 89 to 87 percent. Although these differences may seem small, they would become considerable if the same rates of decrease were to continue over a longer period.

The data from the SPPA and BISG findings reported above are not the only signs of less frequent reading among young adults. Data from an annual, school-based survey of high school seniors called *Monitoring the Future* shows a gradual diminution in the proportion who report reading books, magazines, or newspapers "almost every day," from 62 percent in 1977 to 46 percent in 1988.[31] Thus, evidence from three different survey programs points to the conclusion that a decline in reading is occurring among successive cohorts of young adults in the United States.

A Fluid Situation

Why is literature reading remaining stagnant or even declining, when various demographic factors indicate that it should be increasing? Reasons for the lack of growth are examined at the conclusion of this monograph. We note here, though, that the situation is a fluid one, especially as far as sales of literature are concerned. With so many potential readers in the population, and such a small fraction of them needed to make a bestseller, there could be short-term increases in literature sales even while a long-term decline in literature reading was in progress. Book sales also depend on economic conditions, the popularity of the current crop

TABLE 3. Change in Proportion of Adult Population and Population Subgroups That Have Read Literature, Read Books or Magazines, Read Poetry, and Done Creative Writing in the Last 12 Months, U.S. Adults Aged 18 and Over, 1982 to 1985.

	Literature Readers			All Readers		
All Adults (18+)	1985	1982	Differ- ence	1985	1982	Differ- ence
No. in population (in millions)	95.2	92.5	2.7	146.0	138.0	8.0
% of Adult Pop.	56.0%	56.4%	–0.4%	85.6%	84.1%	1.4%
% of All Readers	65.2%	67.0%	–1.8%	100.0%	100.0%	—
Population Subgroups						
AGE						
Young (18-29)	56.8%	60.9%	–4.1%	87.0%	89.4%	–2.4%
Middle (30-49)	60.8%	59.7%	1.1%	88.6%	87.4%	1.2%
Older (50 +)	50.3%	49.6%	0.7%	81.5%	75.9%	5.6%
GENDER						
Female	63.0%	63.0%	0.0%	88.3%	85.6%	2.7%
Male	48.1%	49.1%	–1.0%	82.7%	81.8%	0.9%
ETHNIC GROUP						
White	59.0%	59.8%	–0.8%	89.9%	86.4%	3.5%
Black	43.0%	42.3%	0.7%	66.3%	71.3%	–5.0%
Hispanic	41.5%	36.4%	5.1%	66.0%	72.2%	–6.2%
Asian, Other	51.9%	50.2%	1.7%	85.3%	80.2%	5.1%
EDUCATION						
Some College	75.4%	77.7%	–2.3%	97.2%	96.6%	0.6%
High School Grad	53.4%	55.4%	–2.0%	85.9%	88.0%	–2.1%
Less than HS	32.6%	31.2%	1.4%	68.4%	63.7%	4.7%
INCOME						
$25K & over	66.5%	69.1%	–2.6%	92.3%	94.2%	–1.9%
$10-25K	51.8%	55.0%	–3.2%	85.3%	85.4%	–0.1%
Under $10K	43.6%	43.2%	0.4%	72.3%	69.6%	2.7%
REGION						
Northeast	57.0%	58.3%	–1.3%	86.4%	84.1%	2.3%
Midwest	56.7%	58.4%	–1.7%	90.3%	88.8%	1.5%
South	50.4%	49.0%	1.4%	80.6%	76.6%	4.0%
West	63.7%	63.9%	–0.2%	87.2%	89.0%	–1.8%
RESIDENCE						
Central City	56.5%	56.5%	0.0%	85.5%	83.4%	2.1%
Suburbs	61.0%	60.2%	0.8%	91.2%	88.5%	2.7%
Non-Metro	48.9%	51.7%	–2.8%	78.4%	78.5%	–0.1%

(continued)

SOURCE: National Endowment for the Arts and U.S. Bureau of the Census, 1982 and 1985 Surveys of Public Participation in the Arts, tabulations by N. Zill and M. Winglee from public use data files.

TABLE 3. (Continued) Change in Proportion of Adult Population and Population Subgroups That Have Read Literature, Read Books or Magazines, Read Poetry, and Done Creative Writing in the Last 12 Months, U.S. Adults Aged 18 and Over, 1982 to 1985.

All Adults (18+)	Poetry Readers			Creative Writers		
	1985	1982	Difference	1985	1982	Difference
No. in population (in millions)	31.8	32.5	−0.7	10.6	10.7	−0.1
% of Adult Pop.	18.6%	19.8%	−1.2%	6.2%	6.5%	−0.3%
% of All Readers	21.8%	23.6%	−1.8%	7.3%	7.8%	−0.5%
Population Subgroups						
AGE						
Young (18-29)	19.7%	24.0%	−4.3%	8.5%	10.5%	−2.0%
Middle (30-49)	20.1%	21.1%	−1.0%	7.6%	6.6%	1.0%
Older (50 +)	17.4%	15.2%	2.2%	3.0%	3.1%	−0.1%
GENDER						
Female	21.5%	23.0%	−1.5%	7.4%	8.1%	−0.7%
Male	16.2%	16.2%	0.0%	4.9%	4.7%	0.2%
ETHNIC GROUP						
White	20.0%	20.5%	−0.5%	6.7%	6.6%	0.1%
Black	13.8%	15.1%	−1.3%	4.5%	5.7%	−1.2%
Hispanic	14.8%	16.9%	−2.1%	4.0%	7.0%	−3.0%
Asian, Other	16.0%	23.1%	−7.1%	2.4%	6.1%	−3.7%
EDUCATION						
Some College	28.1%	31.0%	−2.9%	11.5%	11.6%	−0.1%
High School Grad	14.6%	17.9%	−3.3%	3.8%	4.7%	−0.9%
Less than HS	12.1%	8.0%	4.1%	2.0%	2.6%	−0.6%
INCOME						
$25K & over	22.6%	24.1%	−1.5%	8.0%	7.4%	0.6%
$10-25K	19.6%	18.8%	0.8%	6.4%	6.0%	0.4%
Under $10K	14.1%	16.6%	−2.5%	3.2%	5.5%	−2.3%
REGION						
Northeast	17.1%	19.5%	−2.4%	4.6%	6.5%	−1.9%
Midwest	21.0%	20.7%	0.3%	6.6%	5.5%	1.1%
South	18.5%	17.0%	1.5%	4.6%	5.6%	−1.0%
West	17.0%	23.3%	−6.3%	10.0%	9.4%	0.6%
RESIDENCE						
Central City	18.5%	20.7%	−2.2%	7.5%	8.4%	−0.9%
Suburbs	21.2%	20.0%	1.2%	8.2%	6.6%	1.6%
Non-Metro	16.7%	18.9%	−2.2%	2.8%	4.9%	−2.1%

SOURCE: National Endowment for the Arts and U.S. Bureau of the Census, 1982 and 1985 Surveys of Public Participation in the Arts, tabulations by N. Zill and M. Winglee from public use data files.

of authors and titles, and promotional and marketing factors. Partly because of the positive demographic omens mentioned above, the U.S. Department of Commerce is forecasting healthy growth in the book publishing industry through the early 1990s.[32]

The prospects for literature readership depend on whether the observed declines in reading among young adults continue, and on the balance between the older portion of the population (where literature reading seems to be growing) and the younger portion (where it seems to be declining). The current middle-aged population (who were products of the post-war "baby boom") is relatively large, and the young adult population (who were products of the "birth dearth" years) relatively small. Thus, although there is cause for concern about the long-term future of literature, there is reason for guarded optimism in the short run.

Chapter 2
What the Readers Are Reading

Two studies gathered information not only on whether people had read fiction, poetry, or drama, but also on the specific kinds of works they read. The Arts-Related Trend Study asked respondents for specific examples of works they had read, and classified these according to their literary quality, and how appropriate and contemporary they were. The other study, a survey done for the Book Industry Study Group, did not ask for specific titles, but inquired whether the respondent's reading included various forms and genres of fiction, such as mysteries, romances, science fiction, etc. These studies give a more detailed picture of the kinds of reading Americans are doing, and they permit us to make a rough estimate of the size of the audience for serious, as opposed to popular, literature.

Asking for Titles

The Arts-Related Trend Study (ARTS), a nationwide telephone survey on arts knowledge and participation, was conducted by the Survey Research Center at the University of Maryland in June 1983 and January 1984.[33] The sample interviewed for this study (1,077 adults) was considerably smaller than the samples surveyed in the 1982 and 1985 rounds of the SPPA, and its completion rate (70 percent) was lower. But the study collected illuminating follow-up information on the kinds of arts-related activities reported by the SPPA respondents, including the titles and authors of some of the works of literature that each respondent had read during the previous 12 months. When categorized and tabulated, this sample of works read begins to give us a picture of what people mean when they report that they have read literature recently.

The proportion of respondents reporting that they had read one or more works of fiction, poetry, or drama during the previous 12 months was similar to that found in the 1982 SPPA, although about 4 percentage points lower. In addition to the combined question about reading novels, short stories, poetry, or plays, the University of Maryland surveys asked separately about each of these categories of literature.

Novel Reading

Forty percent of the respondents reported that they had read one or more novels during the last 12 months. When asked to give some examples of novels they had read, however, nearly a quarter of the self-described readers could not come up with the name of a specific book or author, or gave the name of a work that was not a novel, but a biography, self-help book, or other non-fiction title. Another 30 percent named only works of light, popular fiction, such as a "blockbuster" by Judith Krantz or Sidney Sheldon, a horror story by Stephen King, a romance by Victoria Holt, a western by Louis L'Amour, a novelization of one of the "Star Wars" films, etc. Ten percent of the novel readers named a classic work, such as a novel by Dickens, Tolstoy, Henry James, Mark Twain, or Hemingway. Seventeen percent reported reading a contemporary work of some literary merit, such as William Styron's *Sophie's Choice,* Norman Mailer's *Ancient Evenings,* Alice Walker's *The Color Purple,* or John Updike's *Couples.*

In terms of overall percentages, 30 percent of all U.S. adults reported reading novels in the last 12 months and could give at least one name that qualified as a title or author of an actual novel. Only about 11 percent of all adults seemed to have read a work of some literary distinction,* however, and only 7 percent had read a meritorious contemporary work. The latter figure is remarkably close to a figure reported by Peter Mann, namely, that 6 percent of British adults who were found to be reading "modern novels" in the 1981 Euromonitor readership survey in Great Britain.[34]

Short Story Reading

Twenty-eight percent of the respondents to the ARTS survey reported reading short stories during the previous twelve months. However, when asked to recall the authors or titles of some of these stories, or the name of the magazine or book in which the stories appeared, many had difficulty. More than a quarter of the ostensible story readers could not provide any descriptive information about the stories, or gave the titles of inappropriate works. Another 10 percent gave responses that could not be classified. Nearly 45 percent more gave only the name of the magazine in which the story appeared, and many of these magazines were ones which contained non-fiction as well as fiction (e.g., *Reader's Digest, Redbook, Family Circle*), or non-fiction feature stories only (*Newsweek, National Geographic*). Thus, there seemed to be confusion in some respondents' minds as to what the term "short story" signified. Less than 20 percent of the story readers named authors, stories, or anthologies of stories that could be classified as "serious" literature; only 5 percent named contemporary writers or stories of literary merit.

In terms of overall percentages, 20 percent of all U.S. adults reported reading short stories and could give some descriptive information about the stories. But only 5 percent of all adults had read stories that could be ascertained to be of literary quality, and less than two percent had read contemporary short stories of literary value.

---

*Judgments about the literary merit of various works are arguable, of course. The categorizations reported here are those made by the staff of the Maryland Survey Research Center, presumably after some consultation with faculty experts on literature. For the most part, these categorizations seem reasonable, although a perusal of the actual responses, which are listed in an appendix to the survey report, reveals some anomalous classifications and a few coding errors.

Poetry Reading

Fifteen percent of the adults surveyed in the Arts-Related Trends Study reported reading poetry during the past 12 months. This was 5 percentage points lower than the proportion reported in the 1982 SPPA.* When asked to provide the names of poets or poems read, or the title of the magazine or book in which the poems were found, nearly 70 percent of the poetry readers were able to provide some corroborative detail. But almost a quarter gave only the name of a mass-circulation magazine such as *Parade* or *Reader's Digest,* or named examples of less serious forms of verse, such as "Gross Limericks," popular song lyrics, or poems written for children. On the other hand, close to 40 percent of the poetry readers named poets, poems, and/or poetry anthologies of literary distinction, including works by T.S. Eliot, Robert Frost, Emily Dickinson, Carl Sandburg, Ezra Pound, Edgar Allan Poe, Robert W. Service, Henry Wadsworth Longfellow, and William Carlos Williams. Very few of the names or poems mentioned were those of serious living poets, however.

As a proportion of the total population, 10 percent of U.S. adults reported reading poetry and could provide some information on what or where poems were read. Six percent had read poems of clear literary merit, mostly modern or traditional classics. One percent or less had read serious contemporary poetry.

Play Reading

Although only 5 percent of the adults surveyed in the ARTS reported reading a play during the previous 12 months, 91 percent of them could name a specific play or dramatist, or both. Moreover, 80 percent of the authors and works mentioned seemed to have literary merit, although less than 10 percent of them were works of living playwrights. Examples of names or plays mentioned include those of Shakespeare, Shaw, Tennessee Williams, Brecht, Lillian Hellman, Tom Stoppard, and Ntozake Shange. In terms of the total adult population, 5 percent reported reading plays and could

---

*The difference suggests that follow-up questions may have had a suppressing effect on the reporting of literary participation. Because this kind of effect is common in survey research, it is good practice to ask all screening questions before asking any follow-up questions. This was not done in the ARTS survey.

give the name of a specific play or playwright read. Four percent had read drama of literary merit, but less than one percent had read serious contemporary dramas.

Table 4 summarizes the ARTS findings on novel, short story, poetry, and play reading. Unfortunately, the published results do not indicate how much overlap there was across these types of reading, so estimates of the total size of the audience for works of literary merit can only be approximate. Depending on the degree of overlap assumed, the total proportion of people reading works of merit could range from a little more than 10 percent up to 25 percent or more, whereas the proportion reading contemporary works of merit could range from 7 to about 10 percent.

Creative Writing

The ARTS survey also asked more detailed questions than the SPPA about creative writing activity. The initial question was, "In the last 12 months, have you taken any lessons in creative writing or done any creative writing for your own pleasure"? If the respondents indicated that they had, they were asked what types of work they had tried to write (stories, novels, poetry, or plays) and whether they had written anything that had been published. All ARTS respondents were also asked if they felt they were able to do creative writing.

Nine percent of the arts respondents said they had written or taken writing lessons in the last 12 months. This was higher than the 7 percent who reported doing creative writing in the 1982 SPPA, but the comparable SPPA question did not include writing lessons. Poetry writing was the most common form mentioned; it was attempted by 6 percent of adults (or 62 percent of those who did some writing). Work on stories or novels was reported by 4 percent of adults (or 38 percent of the writers). Playwriting, which was reported by one percent of the adults (or 9 percent of the writers), was least common.

Only about a quarter of the writers, or 2 percent of all respondents, said they had had something published. This included publication in relatively informal outlets such as school magazines, organizational newsletters, etc. More than a fifth of all the ARTS

TABLE 4. Proportions of U.S. Adult Population That Report Reading Various Forms of Literature in Last 12 Months, and Proportions Reading Works of Literary Merit, U.S. Adults Aged 18 and Over, 1983-84.

Literary Form	Have Read Works in This Form in Last 12 Months	Can Provide Information About Works Read	Mention Work or Author of Literary Merit	Mention Contemporary Work of Merit
Novels	40%	30%	11%	7%
Short Stories	28%	20%	5%	1%
Poetry	15%	10%	6%	1%
Plays	5%	5%	4%	>1%

SOURCE: Developed from data in: Robinson, John R. et al., *Americans' Participation In The Arts: A 1983-84 Arts-Related Trend Study.* Final Report, College Park, MD: University of Maryland Survey Research Center, 1986.

respondents—22 percent—felt that they had the ability to do creative writing.

Varieties of Fiction

Information about the kinds of works that are read by literature readers was also collected in the 1983 Consumer Research Study on Reading and Book Purchasing conducted for the Book Industry Study Group.[35] Instead of asking for specific titles and authors, the BISG survey inquired about categories of fiction read, covering various genres of novels, as well as short stories, poetry, and drama under the fiction rubric. There was no attempt to evaluate the literary quality of the works. The survey used a six-month reporting period, as opposed to the 12-month period used in the SPPA or ARTS questionnaires. The BISG questions about the types of fiction read were only asked of those who reported reading at least one fiction book during the reference period.

Genre Fiction
    The BISG survey found that the novel was the most widely read form of fiction. However, much of the novel reading was spread across a variety of popular genres that are not usually thought of as "literary," though they occasionally produce individual works or authors of enduring quality. Each genre accounted for between 10 and 40 percent of all fiction readers, or about 4 to 15 percent of all adults. As indicated in Table 5, many readers had read works in more than one genre during the previous six months.

Classics, Historical, and Modern Novels
    The survey also asked about the reading of classic works of fiction, "historical novels," and "modern dramatic novels" that did not fall into one of the genre categories. Classics had been read by 19 percent of fiction readers, or about 7 percent of all adults. Comparable figures for historical novels were 35 percent of fiction readers, or 14 percent of adults, and for modern dramatic novels, 31 percent of fiction readers, or 12 percent of adults. Of course, the latter two categories encompass commercial bestsellers as well as works with serious literary intentions.

TABLE 5. Proportions of U.S. Adult Population That Report Reading Various Forms or Genres of Fiction Books in Last Six Months, U.S. Adults Aged 16 and Over, 1983.

	Have Read Books of This Form or Genre in the Last Six Months	
Literary Form	Percent of All Fiction Readers	Percent of All Adults (16+)
All Forms/Genres	100%	39%
Novels		
Action/Adventure	37%	14%
Mystery/Detective	35%	14%
Historical	35%	14%
Modern Dramatic	31%	12%
Romance (Traditional)	28%	11%
Science Fiction	21%	8%
Spy/Internat. Intrigue	19%	7%
Classics	19%	7%
Fantasy	17%	7%
Romance (Sexy)	13%	5%
Romance (Gothic/Hist.)	13%	5%
Occult/Supernatural	12%	5%
Westerns	10%	4%
War Books	10%	4%
Juvenile/Children's	26%	10%
Short Stories	22%	9%
Humor/Satire	20%	8%
Poetry	11%	4%
Plays	8%	3%

SOURCE: Market Facts, Inc. & Research & Forecasts, Inc. *1983 Consumer Research Study On Reading And Book Purchasing. Vol. I: Focus On Adults.* New York: Book Industry Study Group, Inc., 1984.

Poetry, Short Stories, Drama

The BISG study found that 22 percent of fiction readers had read a book of short stories in the previous six months. Eleven percent had read one or more poetry books and 8 percent, one or more books of plays. As a fraction of all respondents, the proportions were about 9 percent for short stories, 4 percent for poetry, and 3 percent for drama. The latter percentages are in reasonably good agreement with those found in the ARTS survey to have read works of literary merit, especially if the difference in reference periods is taken into account.

Audience Size Reconsidered

The results summarized above indicate that literature experts are correct when they say that the proportion of people who read fine literature is far smaller than the 56 percent who report reading fiction, poetry, or drama in the course of a year. If the SPPA estimate of the number of literature readers were taken at face value, it would mean that literature had a substantially larger audience than most of the other arts. For example, the SPPA estimated that some 95 million people read literature in 1985. This was over two-and-a-half times more than the number projected to have visited art museums (37 million), and over four times more than the estimated number of people who attended classical music performances (22 million). Indeed, the ostensible number of literature readers was nearly as great as the 101 million who reported attending movies within a year. (Interestingly, the combined number of adult trade books and mass market paperbacks sold yearly in the U.S.— some 1.1 billion in 1985—is about the same as the total number of movie tickets sold annually.)[36]

What the ARTS and BISG findings show, however, is that many of the professed literature readers read only genre fiction or sentimental verse, the literary equivalents of TV "shoot-em-ups" and sitcoms, or "Top 40" popular music. The proportion who read serious contemporary literature of all forms in the course of a year seems to be about 7 to 12 percent of the adult population (the 12 percent figure coming from the proportion who reported they had read "modern dramatic novels" in the BISG survey). This would still make the audience for literature comparable to that for some of the other arts, roughly the equivalent of the 16 million people who attend jazz performances or the 20 million who see live drama each year.

At the same time, the size of the audience for literature could be two-to-three times larger, depending on where one draws the line between "entertainment" and "art." If one is prepared to take seriously popular authors, such as horror-story writer Stephen King, poet-illustrator Shel Silverstein, humorist Garrison Keillor, or mystery writer John D. MacDonald, as at least some critics are, then the public for literature might be more like a fifth to a quarter, rather than a tenth, of the adult population. If, on the other hand, one restricted the approved following to those familiar with excellent but not widely known authors, such as poets Adrienne Rich or James Merrill, then the size of the audience for contemporary literature would become minuscule indeed.

A few points should be made here. First, it is difficult to make a precise estimate of the overall size of the literary audience from the ARTS and BISG studies, because their published reports do not contain necessary summary tabulations, and because of ambiguities and flaws in the coding and tabulation procedures used in the studies. It would certainly be desirable to conduct a survey that made more careful use of the follow-up questions developed in these studies, with a larger sample and expert advice on the coding of various works and authors. Such a study, however, would not resolve arguments over what is art and what is mere entertainment.

Second, in attempting to gauge the size of the audience for literature, it does not seem appropriate to limit the audience to those who read serious contemporary works, any more than one would wish to limit one's definition of the audience for classical music to those who attend Steve Reich or Milton Babbitt concerts, or the audience for visual art to those who come out for the latest exhibit at the Hirshhorn or Guggenheim. In each of these publics, there is a substantial segment of followers who stick with time-honored works and are not terribly receptive to the new and challenging. It hardly seems fair or wise to exclude these individuals from the audience counts. Their skeptical judgments about the worth of contemporary writers, composers, and painters will, if past experience is any guide, be supported in many instances by art historians of the future. In other cases, of course, the new and sometimes difficult works of today will become part of tomorrow's established canon.

Third, in estimating the size of the audience for poetry, the distinction between those who read classic works only and those who read contemporary as well as classic literature makes a substantial difference. If one includes those who read well-established poetry, then the ARTS and BISG surveys indicate that the audience for serious poetry is about six percent of the adult population. This is larger than the sizes of the audiences for ballet or opera. On the other hand, if one restricts the audience to those who read contemporary "literary" poetry, then, as noted above, the poetry audience amounts to one percent or less of the population.

Finally, looking at the empty rather than the full portion of the glass, it is striking how many adults there are in the American public who can read, are reasonably educated, and have been exposed to at least some literature in the course of their schooling, but who read nothing or virtually nothing in the way of fiction, poetry, or drama on even an occasional basis. The 1985 SPPA found that at least 44 percent of the adult population had not read a single literary work in the course of a year. The majority of these people—62 percent—were high school graduates, and one in five had some college education. Similarly, the BISG study found that 42 percent of the adult population were non-book readers, in the sense that they had read newspapers or magazines, but not a single fiction or non-fiction book during the previous six months. Unfortunately, as noted earlier, the non-book-reading segment of the population appears to be growing.

Chapter 3
Factors That Affect Literary Participation

There are, from the start, a number of demographic characteristics that affect a person's level of participation in the literary arts.

Education

In the 1985 SPPA data, if someone had not completed high school, the odds were about two-to-one that he or she had not read a novel, short story, poem, or play in the last 12 months. If the person had a high school diploma, then the chances became slightly better than fifty-fifty. But if the person had completed one or more years of college, the odds were three-to-one in favor of him or her being a literature reader.

Obviously, education was not a perfect predictor of literary participation. Some people with relatively little education were regular readers of fiction, poetry, or drama, whereas a significant minority of those with college training did not ordinarily read any works of literature. Nevertheless, of the basic background variables, education was the one most closely correlated with literature reading.

Education was also associated with poetry reading and creative writing, but not as strongly. (Table 6.) The proportion of people who had read or listened to poetry was more than twice as large among the college educated as among those with less than a high school education. And the proportion who had tried to do creative writing was five times greater. But even among those with graduate degrees, only a minority had read any poetry, and an even smaller minority had done any creative writing in the last 12 months.

A person's educational attainment tends to be associated with other social characteristics, such as his or her income level and ethnic background. Thus, when education was combined with these and other factors in an equation, the unique contribution of education to the prediction of literary participation was somewhat diminished.* But education still remained the premier predictor, surpassing income and race, as well as age, sex, and residence. It was also the leading predictor of poetry reading and creative writing.

There are a number of reasons why education should be a good predictor of literary participation. The more years of education a person has had, the more likely it is that he or she has been exposed to literature in school and has had instruction in its appreciation.

In addition, years of educational attainment could be used as a proxy measure for intelligence. More intelligent individuals are more likely to be avid and adept readers, to recognize and enjoy good writing, and to share the interests and concerns of those who write literature. Educated persons are also more likely to be exposed to reviews, magazine and newspaper articles, public television and radio programs, and the recommendations of friends. Finally, more educated persons may feel social pressure to read works of literature in order to be able to converse knowledgeably about them with colleagues and friends.

As noted earlier, the association between educational attainment and literature reading, and the rising levels of general education in the United States, would lead one to expect that the amount of literature reading is increasing. But other influences can over-

---

*Results of the predictive equations, which made use of a technique called logistic regression analysis, are shown in greater detail in the Technical Appendix.

TABLE 6. Relationship Between Education and Income Levels and Literature Reading, Poetry Reading, Creative Writing, and Book or Magazine Reading in Last 12 Months, U.S. Adults Aged 18 and Over, 1985.

	Proportion of Population Group Who...			
	Read Literature	Read Poetry	Did Creative Writing	Read Books, Magazines
ALL ADULTS	56.0%	18.6%	6.2%	85.6%
EDUCATION GROUPS				
Some College	75.4%	28.1%	11.5%	97.2%
High School Grad	53.4%	14.6%	3.8%	85.9%
Less than HS	32.6%	12.1%	2.0%	68.4%
INCOME GROUPS				
$25K & over	66.5%	22.6%	8.0%	92.3%
$10—25K	51.8%	19.6%	6.4%	85.3%
Under $10K	43.6%	14.1%	3.2%	72.3%

SOURCE: National Endowment for the Arts and U.S. Bureau of the Census, 1985 Survey of Public Participation in the Arts, tabulations by N. Zill and M. Winglee from public use data files.

ride the effects of education on social behavior and produce trends that are different from the expected ones. Voting is a good example of this. As with the propensity to read literature, the propensity to vote is positively correlated with educational attainment. But rising education levels have not resulted in increased levels of voter turnout, at least not in recent decades. Moreover, as critics of the educational system are quick to point out, the rise in general education levels has been accompanied by some decay in educational quality. A high school diploma does not necessarily mean as much as it once did in terms of skills mastered and knowledge gained.

Income

Like education, an individual's income level is significantly associated with literary participation. Among persons in the 1985 SPPA who had annual incomes of $25,000 or more, the odds were about two-to-one that they had read a work of fiction, poetry, or drama in the previous twelve months. For those with incomes between $10,000 and $25,000, the odds dropped to just over fifty-fifty. And among those with incomes below $10,000, the chances were about six-to-four against their being literature readers.

Income level was also correlated with the general reading of books and magazines, and with the reading of poetry and creative writing. (Table 6.) However, the relationships between income and poetry reading, and income and creative writing, were considerably weaker than the relationship with overall literature reading. For example, those with incomes of $25,000 and over were only about one-and-a-half times more likely to have read poetry than those with incomes below $10,000.

A person's income is associated with his or her education level and ethnic group, so some of the correlation between income and literary participation could be due to these factors, rather than to income per se. When income was combined with the other demographic factors in a logistic regression equation,* the amount of predictive power contributed by income, over and above that provid-

---

*This equation allows a "better fit" of the data by fitting them into a curve rather than a straight line.

ed by education, turned out to be slight. Income was still a significant, though weak, predictor of overall literature reading, but not of poetry reading or creative writing.

Thus, those with higher incomes are more likely to be literature readers than those with lower incomes, primarily because the former tend to be more educated than the latter. The fact that they also have more money to buy books and more leisure time to enjoy them may also play a role, but apparently not a major one.

Gender

Another basic characteristic that has a bearing on literary participation is a person's gender. If a respondent in the 1985 SPPA was a woman, the odds were nearly two-to-one that she had read a novel, short story, poem, or play in the previous 12 months. For men, by contrast, the odds were less than fifty-fifty. Women were also more likely to have read books and magazines in general, to have read poetry, and to have done creative writing, though all of these relationships were considerably weaker than the association with literature reading. (Table 7.)

When the demographic variables were combined in predictive equations, gender proved to be the second-strongest factor (after education) in separating literature readers and poetry readers from non-readers. It was the fourth-strongest factor (after education, age, and non-metropolitan residence) in differentiating creative writers from non-writers.

In the BISG survey on reading, women were found to be much more likely than men to be frequent book readers. Gender was also associated with the amount of reading done: women were more likely to be readers of fiction, and men of non-fiction. Men were more apt to be readers of newspapers and magazines, but not books. As might be expected, certain genres of fiction, such as romances, had a largely female following, whereas other genres, such as action/adventure stories and science fiction, had readerships that were predominantly male.[37]

It would seem that both cultural and biological factors are at work in accounting for the gender differences in literary participation. As discussed later, there is evidence that girls get more encouragement to read from their parents. But there is also evi-

TABLE 7. Relationship Between Gender and Age/Year of Birth and Literature Reading, Poetry Reading, Creative Writing, and Book or Magazine Reading
in Last 12 Months, U.S. Adults Aged 18 and Over, 1985.

	Proportion of Population Group Who...			
	Read Literature	Read Poetry	Did Creative Writing	Read Books, Magazines
ALL ADULTS	56.0%	18.6%	6.2%	85.6%
GENDER				
Female	63.0%	21.5%	7.4%	88.3%
Male	48.1%	16.2%	4.9%	82.7%
AGE/BIRTH YEAR				
Young (18-29)	56.8%	19.7%	8.5%	87.0%
Middle (30-49)	60.8%	20.1%	7.6%	88.6%
Older (50 +)	50.3%	17.4%	3.0%	81.5%

SOURCE: National Endowment for the Arts and U.S. Bureau of the Census,
1985 Survey of Public Participation in the Arts, tabulations by N.
Zill and M. Winglee from public use data files.

dence of innate differences between the sexes in the development of reading skills and interests. Studies of standardized reading tests given to elementary-school children have found that, on the average, girls read earlier, better, and more than boys do. Girls do not surpass boys in all verbal areas: boys do as well or even slightly better on vocabulary tests. But girls excel on tests of reading proficiency, and fewer girls encounter difficulties in learning to read.[38] Girls also write letters earlier and express more positive attitudes toward reading stories.[39]

For reasons that are not well understood, women lose much of their advantage over men on reading tests by late adolescence and young adulthood.[40] Among college-bound high school students, for example, men score slightly higher than women on the verbal portion of the Scholastic Aptitude Test (SAT), including the reading comprehension subtest. On the other hand, women do slightly better on the Test of Standard Written English that is given as part of the SAT, as well as on the English Composition Achievement Test. Young women in high school and college continue to do more reading than men, especially reading for pleasure, and to know more about literature. Thus, nearly twice as many women as men take the College Board Achievement Test in Literature, and the mean score attained by women is significantly higher than that for men.[41]

It might also be argued that women may be drawn to literature because of a greater interest in human character development and social interaction patterns. In the past, women were raised in a manner that called for sensitivity to other people's feelings and motivations, and for getting one's way through persuasion rather than assertiveness. Obviously, much of literature is concerned with how people behave in various situations and why they act as they do.

It is interesting to speculate about what effects the women's movement has had and will have on female involvement with literature. Certainly, the drive for women's rights has helped to draw attention to outstanding women writers, and to open more opportunities for women in the publication and promotion of literature. One would also think, given the changes that women as a group have been undergoing, that many would want to read or write about their experiences and feelings in fictional, poetic, or dramatic forms. Whenever norms and values are in flux, literature has a special role to play. Literature can be a vehicle for exploring new patterns of behavior and interaction. It can provide fictional characters that serve as role models to real people going through similar struggles. And it can give voice to both the exhilaration and the frustrations that many pioneers experience. Although many of the best-known feminist authors, such as Betty Friedan and Germaine Greer, are non-fiction writers, feminist issues and themes appear in a broad range of contemporary fiction, including the works of writers as disparate as Mary Gordon, Erica Jong, and Francine du Plessix Gray.

Even the emergence of a new type of popular romance novels with a more overtly sexual content can be at least partly attributed to the women's movement, in the sense that the movement has made it easier for women to be open about their sexuality. However, as more women become involved in traditionally male career paths, one wonders whether their reading patterns will become more like the instrumental, non-fiction oriented reading of men.

Age

The year in which a person was born has relevance to literary participation, both because it represents where the individual is in his or her life cycle and because it indicates the historical period in which the person was raised. If literary participation patterns are changing over time, the change should be reflected in differences between age groups. The problem is in disentangling historical change from aging effects. This is not completely possible with data from a single point in time, or even from two closely spaced surveys. Some reasonable inferences can usually be drawn about what is occurring, however, depending on the pattern of change actually observed.

The wide range of birth years represented in the 1985 SPPA was broken down into three broad groups: young adults (ages 18-29, or birth years 1956-1967); middle-aged adults (ages 30-49, or birth years 1936-1955); and older adults (ages 50 and older, or birth years 1935 and earlier). When this division was made, a relatively weak relationship was found between age and literary participation: participation declined from the middle to the older years. The proportion reading literature, for example, decreased from 61 percent in the middle years to 50 percent in the older years. Similar declines were observed in creative writing, general reading, and poetry reading, although the last difference was very slight. (Table 7.) Differences between the middle-aged and younger groups were so small as not to be statistically significant, but were generally in the direction of the middle-aged reading more than young adults. Creative writing was an exception, being higher in the young group, but by very little.

Because education levels have been rising over time, age and year of birth are correlated with educational attainment. Older groups have lower education levels, on the average, than younger age groups. Age and birth year are also somewhat correlated with income levels (because middle-aged individuals tend to earn more money than younger or older people) and with the sexual composition of the group (because women tend to live longer than men). When education and other demographic variables were entered into predictive equations along with age (which was treated as a continuous variable in the equations), the unique contribution of age to the process of differentiating readers from non-readers was essentially eliminated.

Thus, the decline in literature reading with age can be explained by the correlation between birth year and education level. Older people read less than younger ones, not because they are older (and hence more infirm, or less energetic, or some such), but primarily because they are less educated. This finding has an important implication for future consumption. Future cohorts of older Americans, being more educated than the senior citizens of today, will presumably be reading more literature. It may also be that the total volume of literature reading will increase, although the increase in reading among the elderly may be offset by declines in reading among young adults.

The apparent negative effect of age on literary participation was not eliminated in the equation that differentiated creative writers from non-writers. Although the effect of age was still quite weak, it was the second-best predictor in the equation, after education. This suggests that age as such has some debilitating or discourag-

ing effect on the production of imaginative writing. In her book
The Coming of Age, Simone de Beauvoir concludes that great age
is generally not conducive to literary creation, especially to the
writing of novels. She attributes this to the waning with age of the
"alacrity" and strength that imaginative writing requires. But de
Beauvoir also mentions notable exceptions to the rule, famous
authors like Sophocles, Cervantes, Voltaire, Victor Hugo, and Henry
James, who created some of their finest works in later life.[42]

The decline in amateur writing with age seems unfortunate
because older individuals, having experienced more, should have
more to write about. Once retired, they also have more time to
practice the craft of writing. Perhaps, as attitudes about what is
possible and appropriate for older people to do change, the decline in writing associated with increased age will change as well.

Race/Ethnicity

Blacks and Hispanics are less likely to have read literature than
whites. The 1985 SPPA data show that the odds on someone who
was Black or Hispanic having read a novel, short story, poem, or
play in the previous 12 months were about 40-60 against. For non-
minority whites, on the other hand, the odds were nearly 60-40
in favor. In addition, whites were about 50 percent more likely than
Blacks or Hispanics to have read poetry or done some creative writing. (Table 8.) The rates for individuals from other minority groups
(predominantly Asians) generally fell between those of whites and
Blacks and Hispanics.

Educational Handicaps. Especially among older adults,
minority ethnic status is associated with lower educational attainment and income levels in our society, despite the dramatic improvement in educational and employment opportunities for
minorities in the last three decades. Substantial fractions of Black
and Hispanic adults are either illiterate or "aliterate." Many
Hispanic-Americans and some Asian-Americans are literate in their
native languages, but not in English. A finding from the 1985 SPPA
illustrates these problems: one third of Blacks and Hispanics had
not read any kind of book or magazine in the last year. The comparable proportion among white adults was one tenth.

But when education, income, and other demographic factors

TABLE 8. Relationship Between Ethnic Group Membership and Literature Reading, Poetry Reading, Creative Writing, and Book or Magazine Reading in Last 12 Months, U.S. Adults Aged 18 and Over, 1985.

	Proportion of Population Group Who...			
	Read Literature	Read Poetry	Did Creative Writing	Read Books, Magazines
ALL ADULTS	56.0%	18.6%	6.2%	85.6%
ETHNIC GROUPS				
Whites	59.0%	20.0%	6.7%	89.9%
Blacks	43.0%	13.8%	4.5%	66.3%
Hispanics	41.5%	14.8%	4.0%	66.0%
Asians, Others	51.9%	16.0%	2.4%	85.3%

SOURCE: National Endowment for the Arts and U.S. Bureau of the Census, 1985 Survey of Public Participation in the Arts, tabulations by N. Zill and M. Winglee from public use data files.

were entered along with race into equations predicting literary participation, the predictive power of race was considerably reduced. (Because of the relatively small size of the Hispanic and Asian subsamples, only a variable differentiating Black from non-Black respondents was entered into the predictive equations.) In the equations differentiating poetry readers from non-readers, and creative writers from non-writers, race added nothing to the prediction. In the equation predicting overall literature reading, race remained a significant, though weak, predictor. Similar results were obtained in analyses with the data from the 1982 SPPA.

Socialization and skill differences. Minority individuals are less likely to have been exposed to literature as children. Educational research studies have found that minority children, especially Hispanics, tend to have fewer reading materials in their homes than non-minority youngsters, and are less apt to have been read to by their parents.[43] Consistent with this, Hispanic adults in the SPPA reported that their parents generally had not encouraged them to read books that were not required for school. In addition, the quality of the formal education many minority individuals receive is inferior to that received by the typical non-minority individual. Thus, in the SPPA, fewer Black and Hispanic respondents reported that they had been exposed to lessons in creative writing.

Furthermore, even though the basic reading skills and educational attainment levels of minority young people have risen substantially since the 1960s, standardized tests still show that the reading proficiency of both Black and Hispanic youths lags behind that of non-minority youths with equivalent years of education. In 1988, for example, the National Assessment of Educational Progress found that only about one-quarter of Black or Hispanic 17-year-olds could read on an adept level, whereas nearly half of the white 17-year-olds were adept readers.[44]

Availability of minority literature. In addition to these educational barriers, there is the question of the availability of fiction, poetry, and drama that is of interest to minority adults and reflects their concerns and cultural traditions. The works of a few contemporary Black writers, such as Alex Haley, Toni Morrison, Ntozake Shange, Alice Walker, and August Wilson, have received widespread public attention in recent years. And some older Black writers like Langston Hughes, James Baldwin, Ralph Ellison, Richard Wright, and Lorraine Hansberry, have received recognition because of the enduring value of their work, and as a result of "Black History Month" and other efforts to raise public consciousness about the contributions of Blacks to American culture. The sad truth, though, is that many Black young people are ignorant of these authors and their works. Moreover, although the situation is far better than it was in the past, it could hardly be said that there is as yet an extensive body of literary works by and for Black Americans.

The situation is worse for Hispanic Americans. For one thing, the Hispanic community is not a unified whole. It is divided into Mexican-Americans, Puerto Ricans, Cuban-Americans, those from Spain, and those from the different Central or South American countries. Each of these groups has somewhat different traditions and concerns. Most Hispanic-American authors are not well known within their own communities and are virtually unknown to a broader audience. Although there has been a surge of interest in Latin American writers of late, this has had little carryover to Hispanic authors writing in the U.S. Many of the latter continue to have difficulty getting their works published and disseminated to appropriate audiences.

Residence

There is significant variation in literary participation across different regions of the country and from urban to rural communities. These differences, however, are relatively modest and are probably due mostly to differences in average educational level across areas, or to the likely tendency of people who have literary inclinations to prefer living in some areas over others.

Regional variations. In the data from the 1985 SPPA, the odds that someone who lived in the West had read a novel, short story, poem, or play in the last 12 months were almost two-to-one. By contrast, the odds that someone from the South had done so were only about 50-50. The odds for residents of the Northeast and Midwest were just slightly better than those for the nation as a whole. (Table 9.) A similar pattern of regional variation was visible in the data from the 1982 SPPA. Poetry reading and creative writing

TABLE 9. Relationship Between Region and Metropolitan Residence and Literature Reading, Poetry Reading, Creative Writing, and Book or Magazine Reading in Last 12 Months, U.S. Adults Aged 18 and Over, 1985.

| | Proportion of Population Group Who... | | | |
	Read Literature	Read Poetry	Did Creative Writing	Read Books, Magazines
ALL ADULTS	56.0%	18.6%	6.2%	85.6%
REGION				
Northeast	57.0%	17.1%	4.6%	86.4%
Midwest	56.7%	21.0%	6.6%	90.3%
South	50.4%	18.5%	4.6%	80.6%
West	63.7%	17.0%	10.0%	87.2%
RESIDENCE				
Central City	56.5%	18.5%	7.5%	85.5%
Suburbs	61.0%	21.2%	8.2%	91.2%
Non-Metro	48.9%	16.7%	2.8%	78.4%

SOURCE: National Endowment for the Arts and U.S. Bureau of the Census, 1985 Survey of Public Participation in the Arts, tabulations by N. Zill and M. Winglee from public use data files.

showed weaker and somewhat different patterns of regional variation, although the West was still the leading region as far as the
proportion doing creative writing was concerned. It was not possible to evaluate the predictive power of region after other factors
were controlled because the Census Bureau does not release both
geographic identifiers and household socioeconomic data in the
same public use files.

Urban-rural variations. The 1985 SPPA data showed that the
odds were about 60-40 that someone living in the suburbs of the
major metropolitan areas had read a work of literature in the previous 12 months. By contrast, the odds for a person living outside
of the metropolitan areas were less than 50-50. Residents of non-
metropolitan areas were also below average in rates of general reading, creative writing, and poetry reading, although the differences
with respect to poetry were relatively slight. Residents of the central cities of metropolitan areas were close to the national average
on each of the participation variables. Similar patterns of urban-
rural variation were found in the data from the 1982 SPPA.

The metropolitan residential factor was entered into predictive equations by means of two variables, one identifying those who
lived in central cities, and the other, those who lived in non-
metropolitan areas. Only the latter added significantly to the predictions. When education, income, age, and other demographic variables were taken into account, the contribution of non-metropolitan
residence was considerably reduced. Residence was, however, the
third-strongest predictor of creative writing (after education and
age). It was also a significant though weak predictor of overall literature reading. Thus, most of the negative effect of non-metropolitan
residence on literary participation is due to other characteristics
of the residents, such as their education levels and ages. There is,
however, some residual effect or correlate of residence that is not
accounted for by the demographic characteristics of the residents.

Predicting Participation from Demographics
In sum, the likelihood that a person will or will not be a reader of literature is significantly related to a number of basic background characteristics, the foremost being his or her education level.
While gender, age, ethnic background, income level, and place

of residence are also related, they tell only a limited amount about the person's propensity to read. Other, more specific factors in the individual's history and current life situation, such as parental encouragement to read, also come into play, and are examined in the next section. But first, it is useful to see how well literary participation can be predicted when the basic background characteristics are combined into predictive equations.

Literature reading. Five variables were entered into the equation for discriminating literature readers from non-readers. (In this case, as in each of the later equations, differing numbers of variables were relevant and entered into the equation.) For the 1985 SPPA, education and gender were the predominant predictors, with income, race, and non-metropolitan residence adding tiny but statistically significant increments of predictive power. The equation was able to classify 68 percent of the survey respondents correctly. (Bear in mind that one would get about a 50 percent correct classification by simply alternating between predictions of "reader" and "non-reader," and 56 percent correct by predicting that everyone was a literature reader.) There was also a moderately good correlation between the predicted probability of being a reader and the actual response. The model did somewhat better at identifying those who were readers (71 percent correct) than those who were not (63 percent correct). An almost identical equation and similar predictive results were obtained with the data from the 1982 SPPA.

Poetry reading. Only two variables—education and gender— were entered into the equation for differentiating poetry readers from non-readers. The equation classified 75 percent of the respondents correctly, but given the relatively small proportion of poetry readers in the survey, one would get about 80 percent correct by predicting that no one had read a poem. Of course, the latter strategy would lead to a complete misidentification of those who actually did read poetry (a zero "hit rate"). On the other hand, the equation correctly identified 35 percent of those who had read poetry and 83 percent of those who had not. The rank-order correlation between predicted probability and response ($r = .32$) was moderate, but weaker than that obtained with the literature reading equation. The equation and predictive accuracy obtained with the 1982 data were similar, although the additional (but weak) predictors of age and non-metropolitan residence figured into the 1982 equation.

Creative writing. Four variables were entered into the equation for discriminating creative writers from non-writers. Once again, education was the leading predictor, but this time age was the second-best predictor. Non-metropolitan residence and gender also figured into the equation. The equation classified 92 percent of the respondents correctly, about the same overall proportion correct that one would get by predicting that no one had done any creative writing in the last 12 months. However, the equation was able to identify correctly 21 percent of the actual writers, as well as 95 percent of the non-writers. The rank-order correlation between predicted probability and actual response ($r = .54$) was moderately good. The predictive accuracy obtained with the 1982 SPPA data was nearly identical, and the equation similar, although central city residence (rather than non-metropolitan residence) and income figured into the 1982 equation.

Socialization and Training

Early Encouragement of Reading

One factor that markedly increases an adult's chances of being a regular reader of literature is having grown up in a family where reading was practiced and encouraged. Studies of academic achievement in children consistently find that the parents' education level and the academic orientation of the home are among the best predictors of how well a child will do in school.[45] Aspects of the home environment that correlate with achievement include the number of books and other reading materials in the home, whether the child was read to regularly, and whether the parents encouraged the child to read books not required for school. Similarly, the SPPA has found that one's participation in the arts as an adult is correlated with the education level of one's parents and with recollections of having been exposed to the arts by one's parents when one was a child.[46] Of the various relationships between childhood socialization indicators and measures of adult arts participation that are covered in the survey, those involving participation in literature are among the strongest.

Parents' education level. The SPPA asked respondents to report the highest grade or year of regular school their fathers and mothers had completed according to six categories ranging from "7th grade or less" to "completed college (4+ years)." Although 17 percent of the respondents in the 1985 survey could not recall their father's education level and 13 percent could not recall their mother's, most were able to come up with at least an approximation. For the purpose of the analyses reported here, the higher of the two education levels was used; if only one parent's education level was known, it was used. The proportion of respondents whose parents attained each education level is shown in Table 10.

Respondents with college-educated parents were considerably more likely to be literature readers than those whose parents had less than a high school education. If the respondent's parents were college graduates, the odds on the person having read literature in the past 12 months were about four-to-one. However, if the parents had only an elementary school education, the odds were reduced to less than 50-50. Parent education was also related to the chances of having read poetry or done creative writing, though not as strongly.

As might be expected, the relationships between the literary participation measures and parent's education were not as strong as those with the respondent's own educational attainment. This is partly because there is less recall error in the measure of the respondent's own education. But it is mainly because the respondent's education is a better indicator of his or her intelligence and educational experiences. Of course, parent's education and own education are significantly correlated. Parent's education was also related to the respondent's year of birth (with respondents born in more recent years having better educated parents) and ethnic group (with Black and Hispanic respondents having less educated parents than non-minority respondents).

Parental encouragement of reading. SPPA participants were asked: "Did your parents—or other adult members of the household—encourage you to read books which were not required for school or religious studies: often, occasionally, or never?" Of those in the 1985 SPPA, 37 percent reported that their parents encouraged them to read often; 29 percent were encouraged occa-

TABLE 10. Relationship Between Parent Education Level and Literature Reading, Poetry Reading, Creative Writing, and Book or Magazine Reading in Last 12 Months, and Proportion of Adults with Parents at Each Education Level, U.S. Adults Aged 18 and Over, 1982 and 1985.

| | Proportion of Population Group Who... | | | |
	Read Literature	Read Poetry	Did Creative Writing	Read Books, Magazines
		1982 Data		
ALL ADULTS	56.4%	19.8%	6.5%	84.1%
PARENT'S EDUCATION				
College grad plus	81.0%	35.9%	13.0%	97.9%
Some college	76.0%	33.4%	12.0%	96.8%
High school grad.	64.9%	22.0%	9.1%	91.1%
Some high school	56.9%	20.0%	4.6%	82.1%
Grade school only	43.1%	14.4%	2.6%	71.5%

	1985 Data	Proportion of Adults with Parents at Each Education Level	
ALL ADULTS	56.0%		
		1985	1982
PARENT'S EDUCATION			
College grad plus	78.3%	15.4%	15.0%
Some college	78.3%	12.2%	9.4%
High school grad.	61.7%	35.2%	34.2%
Some high school	50.8%	10.4%	11.7%
Grade school only	42.9%	26.7%	29.7%
		100.0%	100.0%

SOURCE: National Endowment for the Arts and U.S. Bureau of the Census, 1982 and 1985 Surveys of Public Participation in the Arts, tabulations by N. Zill and M. Winglee from public use data files.

sionally; and 34 percent, never.

The relationship between parental encouragement to read and adult literature reading was quite strong, stronger even than the relationship between the respondent's education level and literature reading. For persons who were frequently encouraged to read as children, the odds were nearly four-to-one that they had read a novel, short story, poem, or play in the last 12 months. For those who were never encouraged to read, on the other hand, the odds were more than two-to-one against them having read literature in the last year. Parental encouragement was also related to the chances of having done other types of reading or creative writing, though not as strongly. (Table 11.)

As would be expected, reports that the parents encouraged the respondent to read were related to the parents' education level. If the parents were college graduates, 61 percent of the respondents said they were often encouraged to read. On the other hand, if the parents had an elementary education, only 25 percent were often encouraged to read, and more than half were never encouraged. Parental encouragement also varied across ethnic groups. It was less common among Hispanics than among Blacks, whites, or Asians. Only 20 percent of Hispanic respondents reported that they were often encouraged to read, and 54 percent said they were never encouraged. (Table 12.)

Women were more likely than men to report that they had been encouraged to read as children (42 percent of the women, as opposed to 32 percent of the men). Parental encouragement also varied by year of birth, with those born more recently being considerably more apt to have been encouraged as children. Only 26 percent of those born in 1910 or earlier reported that they had often been encouraged to read, and less than half had been encouraged even occasionally. By contrast, 40 percent or more of those born since World War II were given frequent encouragement, and 70 percent or more received at least occasional encouragement.

Limitations of the evidence of socialization effects. The data just reported seem to provide evidence that the encouragement of reading in childhood helps to form an abiding habit of reading for pleasure and enlightenment. The differences across groups in parental encouragement are also generally consistent with the group

TABLE 11. Relationship Between Socialization Factors (Parental Encourage-
ment of Reading, Respondent's Exposure to Creative Writing Lessons) and
Literature Reading, Poetry Reading, Creative Writing, and Book or Magazine
Reading in Last 12 Months, U.S. Adults Aged 18 and Over, 1982 and 1985.

	Proportion of Population Group Who...			
	Read Literature	Read Poetry	Did Creative Writing	Read Books, Magazines
	—1985—		—1982—	
ALL ADULTS	56.0%	19.8%	6.5%	84.1%
PARENTS ENCOURAGED READING				
Often	79.0%	32.8%	10.4%	94.6%
Occasionally	57.0%	17.1%	6.0%	87.6%
Never	32.0%	9.1%	2.8%	64.8%
R HAD CREATIVE WRITING LESSONS*				
Yes	88.2%	46.8%	25.2%	98.5%
No	49.6%	15.2%	2.7%	79.9%

*R denotes respondent.

SOURCE: National Endowment for the Arts, and U.S. Bureau of the Census,
1982 and 1985 Surveys of Public Participation in the Arts, tabulations by N. Zill and M. Winglee from public use data files.

TABLE 12. Frequency with Which Parents Encouraged Reading by Parent Education Level, Year of Respondent's Birth, Ethnic Group, and Gender, U.S. Adults Aged 18 and Over, 1985.

| | Parents Encouraged Reading... | | | |
	Often	Occasionally	Never	Total
		Percent Distributions		
ALL ADULTS	37.3%	29.0%	33.7%	100.0%
PARENT'S EDUCATION				
College graduate	60.5%	28.0%	11.5%	100.0%
Some college	52.7%	30.4%	16.8%	99.9%
High school grad.	40.7%	36.1%	23.2%	100.0%
Some high school	35.4%	32.8%	31.8%	100.0%
Grade school only	24.9%	23.6%	51.4%	99.9%
YEAR OF R'S BIRTH*				
1956-1967	40.1%	32.3%	27.6%	100.0%
1936-1955	38.6%	32.8%	28.6%	100.0%
1935 or earlier	33.6%	22.4%	44.0%	100.0%
ETHNIC GROUP				
White	38.8%	29.7%	31.5%	100.0%
Black	37.9%	27.1%	34.9%	99.9%
Hispanic	20.2%	25.5%	54.3%	100.0%
Asian, other	43.6%	22.9%	33.5%	100.0%
GENDER				
Female	42.3%	26.9%	30.8%	100.0%
Male	31.7%	31.3%	37.0%	100.0%

*R denotes respondent.

SOURCE: National Endowment for the Arts and U.S. Bureau of the Census, 1985 Survey of Public Participation in the Arts, tabulations by N. Zill and M. Winglee from public use data files.

differences in literary participation that were reported earlier. A few caveats are in order, however. To begin with, the evidence on socialization effects is based on retrospective recall of parental education levels and encouragement, rather than on observations or reports made at the time. With such distant recall, there is the possibility that memory is distorting the past to make it consistent with present behavior, or that reports of literature reading and parental encouragement are related because of common response bias. Thus, to be properly cautious, the evidence should really be seen as suggestive rather than definitive.

Furthermore, even if the relationships between parental characteristics and adult literary participation prove to be genuine, the mechanism involved might be at least partly genetic, rather than wholly environmental. The same criticism applies here as has been applied to studies of family influences on children's school achievement.[47] High parental education levels and encouragement of reading could be seen as markers of high IQ, or of literary talent and interest, which may be passed on to the child as much or more through shared genes as through a nurturing home environment.

It should also be noted that while growing up in a home where parents read a lot and reading materials are readily available is conducive to later literary participation, it is not essential. In the past, when educational opportunities were more limited, many individuals who became well-read adults were raised by parents who could not or did not read themselves. It does seem possible for schools and libraries to make up for what the home does not provide. On the other hand, the findings on parental encouragement of reading suggest that, in trying to teach young people to develop a lifelong appreciation for literature, the emotional context in which the learning occurs is important.

Creative Writing Classes

In addition to family influences, adult reading habits are shaped by the formal training a person has received. The SPPA found that adults who had taken lessons in music, art, acting, ballet, or classes in music or art appreciation, were more likely to attend or take part in related artistic activities than people who had not taken lessons or classes.[48] As described below, a similar relationship was obtained between creative writing classes and literary participation. Here again, the issue arises of whether having taken a class is a cause of later participation or merely an indicator that the person has a predilection for the subject. Probably both mechanisms contribute to the observed relationships.

Respondents in the arts surveys were asked whether they had ever taken lessons or a class in creative writing. Those who said they had were asked to specify in which of four age ranges (elementary school, secondary school, college, later adulthood) the classes were taken. In the 1985 SPPA, 18 percent of all adults said they had taken creative writing lessons or classes at some point. Most had received such instruction when they were of high school or college age. (Table 13.) Only 3 percent had taken writing classes when they were 25 or older. Practically identical proportions were obtained in the 1982 SPPA.

Creative writing lessons were less common than music lessons (which had been taken by nearly half of all adults), crafts lessons (about a third had received these at some point), or visual arts lessons (one quarter had taken these). They were about as frequent as music appreciation or art appreciation classes, and more common than acting or ballet lessons (each of which had been taken by about one tenth of all respondents).

If the person had taken a lesson or class in creative writing, the odds were nearly nine-to-one that he or she had read a novel, short story, poem, or play in the last 12 months. For those who had not taken such a class, the odds were about 50-50. Adults who had taken writing classes were also more likely to have read poetry and books and magazines in general. (Table 11.) As might be expected, there was a moderately strong relationship between taking writing classes and doing creative writing. Although only a quarter of those who had ever taken a class in creative writing had done such writing within the last year, this rate was eight times higher than that for adults who had not taken such courses.

Significant correlations between writing instruction and literary participation were found no matter at what ages the writing classes had been taken. However, courses taken in the college years (18-24) seemed to make slightly more of a difference than those at other ages.

TABLE 13. Number and Proportion of Adults Who Had Creative Writing Lessons at Various Ages, U.S. Adults Aged 18 and Over, 1982 and 1985.

	Number		Proportion	
	1985	1982	1985	1982
Age at Which Lessons Were Taken				
ALL AGES	30.6 mil.	29.7 mil.	18%	18%
Less than 12 yrs.	1.6	1.3	1%	1%
12-17 years	14.6	12.7	9%	8%
18-24 years	16.5	16.6	10%	10%
25 yrs. or more	5.0	5.0	3%	3%

SOURCE: National Endowment for the Arts and U.S. Bureau of the Census, 1982 and 1985 Surveys of Public Participation in the Arts, tabulations from public use data files.

The more education a person had, the more likely he or she was to have taken a course in creative writing. Nearly 40 percent of those with some college education had done so, as contrasted to about 10 percent of those who stopped at high school, and only 3 percent of those who did not complete high school. Writing training was also more common among those with more educated parents and parents who had encouraged reading. (Table 14.) The chances of having had formal training in creative writing as part of one's education have increased markedly in this century. Only 3 percent of those born in 1910 or earlier received such instruction, as opposed to about 15 percent of those born in the late 1930s or early 1940s, and nearly 30 percent of those born since the mid-1950s. Non-Hispanic white respondents were twice as likely to have received some creative writing training as Black or Asian respondents, and five times more likely than Hispanic respondents. Women were slightly more likely than men to have taken such a course.

Current Life Style

It seems plausible that people's literature reading habits are influenced by major aspects of their daily lives, such as their jobs, marital situations, and family responsibilities. What people do for a living shapes their interest, affects the amount of time and money they have for reading and book purchasing, and exposes them to other people who may encourage or discourage certain types of reading. Similarly, a person's marital status and family situation have effects on interests, discretionary time and money, and exposure to different types of people. Job, marital, and family circumstances also have a good deal to do with a person's need for stimulation, solace, or escape.

As shown below, there were indeed associations in the arts survey data between literature reading and aspects of daily life. The associations proved to be weaker than one might expect, however, especially after controlling for related factors such as education, income, age, and gender. These findings suggest that literature reading is a fairly robust habit that can persist in the face of time pressures and competition from other activities. The other side of

TABLE 14. Proportion of Adults Who Have Ever Taken Creative Writing Lessons by Respondent's Education Level, Year of Birth, Ethnic Group, Gender, Parent's Education Level, and Parental Encouragement of Reading, U.S. Adults Aged 18 and Over, 1985.

	Have Had Lessons In Creative Writing:		
	Yes	No	Total
	Percent Distributions		
ALL ADULTS	18.0%	82.0%	100.0%
EDUCATION LEVEL			
Some college	38.7%	61.3%	100.0%
High school graduate	10.6%	89.4%	100.0%
Less than high school	2.6%	97.4%	100.0%
YEAR OF R'S BIRTH			
1956-1967	28.4%	71.6%	100.0%
1936-1955	20.1%	79.9%	100.0%
1935 or earlier	7.5%	92.5%	100.0%
ETHNIC GROUP			
White	20.4%	79.6%	100.0%
Black	12.1%	87.9%	100.0%
Hispanic	4.1%	95.9%	100.0%
Asian, other	9.0%	91.0%	100.0%
GENDER			
Female	19.0%	81.0%	100.0%
Male	16.9%	83.1%	100.0%
PARENT'S EDUCATION			
College graduate	40.9%	59.1%	100.0%
Some college	36.2%	63.8%	100.0%
High school graduate	19.7%	80.3%	100.0%
Some high school	11.3%	88.7%	100.0%
Grade school only	5.1%	94.9%	100.0%
PARENTS ENCOURAGED READING			
Often	32.7%	67.3%	100.0%
Occasionally	14.4%	85.6%	100.0%
Never	5.7%	94.3%	100.0%

SOURCE: National Endowment for the Arts and U.S. Bureau of the Census, 1985 Survey of Public Participation in the Arts, tabulations by N. Zill and M. Winglee from public use data files.

this coin is that those who are non-readers of literature do not suddenly take it up when placed in circumstances that would seem to give them the opportunity to do so.

Employment and Student Status

The Survey of Public Participation in the Arts collected information about whether the respondent was currently employed, and, if so, at what job and for how many hours per week. The respondent's current employment status was significantly related to all types of reading surveyed, as well as to creative writing. (Table 15.)

In general, those in the labor force (i.e., those working or looking for paid work) were more likely than those not in the labor force to have read literature. Students were a notable exception to this rule. They showed the highest rates of literary participation of all the employment groups. For students in the 1985 SPPA, for example, the odds were about three-to-one that they had read fiction, poetry, or drama in the last 12 months. More than a third had read poems and nearly a fifth had done some creative writing in that period.

Of course, the high participation rates of students are partly due to their being required to read works of literature for courses they are taking. In addition, students tend to be immersed in the world of books and to associate with others who read, recommend, and talk about books. What many will find remarkable about the SPPA findings, however, is not that students' reading rates are so high, but that they are not higher.

Of men and women in the labor force, those who worked part-time had somewhat higher rates of literary participation than those who worked full-time. Those who had a job but were not at work (because of illness, maternity leave, a labor dispute, etc.) also had above-average rates of literature reading, but not of poetry reading or writing. These differences support the notion that having more non-work time available results in more reading of literature. However, people who work part-time are more likely to be female and younger than those who work full-time. Thus, the factors of gender and age contribute to the observed differences as well.

In contrast, those who were unemployed (i.e., without jobs

TABLE 15. Relationship Between Current Employment Status and Literature Reading, Poetry Reading, Creative Writing, and Book or Magazine Reading in Last 12 Months, U.S. Adults Aged 18 and Over, 1985.

	Proportion of Population Group Who...			
	Read Literature	Read Poetry	Did Creative Writing	Read Books, Magazines
ALL ADULTS	56.0%	18.6%	6.2%	85.6%
CURRENT EMPLOYMENT STATUS				
In Labor Force				
Working full time	56.0%	17.8%	7.0%	88.5%
Working part time	61.0%	29.2%	10.1%	90.0%
With job, not at work	64.5%	19.2%	4.8%	88.2%
Unemployed	50.5%	13.3%	3.9%	76.7%
Not In Labor Force				
Student	74.5%	35.3%	19.2%	93.6%
Keeping house	55.4%	16.4%	3.2%	83.5%
Retired, other	49.1%	17.5%	2.5%	76.5%
Disabled	33.7%	14.4%	0.0%	67.2%

SOURCE: National Endowment for the Arts and U.S. Bureau of the Census, 1985 Survey of Public Participation in the Arts, tabulations by N. Zill and M. Winglee from public use data files.

and/or looking for work) showed below–average levels of literary participation and reading in general. In this case, the factor of time available to read was apparently negated by the generally lower education and income levels, and higher concentrations of ethnic minorities among the unemployed. Lower education levels were also the dominant factor in the below-average reading and writing rates shown by those who had retired from the labor force.

Those who were full-time homemakers had average rates of literature reading, about the same as those who worked full-time at paid jobs. Given that most of the homemakers were women, however, the literary participation rates were lower than would be expected. The demands of homemaking and childrearing may have played a role here.

The small group that was not in the labor force because they were disabled showed the lowest rates of literary participation. This group had high proportions of older members with little education and members of minority ethnic groups. In addition, some of the people in this group had disabilities that made it difficult or impossible for them to read.

Occupational Group

The type of occupation at which a person worked showed a moderately strong relationship with literature reading. White collar workers were generally above average in their reading habits, whereas blue collar workers were below average. For those in professional occupations, such as medicine, law, and college teaching, for example, the odds were about three-to-one that they had read a work of literature in the past 12 months. For sales and clerical workers, the odds were about two-to-one. On the other hand, for those in the skilled crafts, such as electricians, machinists, mechanics, and tool and die makers, the odds were about six-to-four against their having read literature. And for laborers, the odds were two-to-one against. Service workers, such as waiters, barbers, dental assistants, and flight attendants, were intermediate. The odds that they had read some literature were slightly better than 50-50, about the same as the national average. Similar relationships were found with poetry reading and creative writing. (Table 16.)

Of course, a person's occupation is closely related to his or

TABLE 16. Relationship Between Occupational Class and Literature Reading, Poetry Reading, Creative Writing, and Book or Magazine Reading in Last 12 Months, U.S. Adults Aged 18 and Over, 1985.

	Proportion of Population Group Who...			
	Read Literature	Read Poetry	Did Creative Writing	Read Books, Magazines
ALL ADULTS	56%	19%	6%	86%
	Observed Proportions			
OCCUPATIONAL CLASS				
Professional	76%	34%	19%	98%
Managerial	71%	22%	11%	93%
Sales, Clerical	67%	22%	5%	94%
Service Workers	54%	21%	11%	86%
Craftsmen	42%	13%	3%	86%
Operatives	37%	9%	2%	68%
Laborers	36%	7%	0%	81%
	Adjusted Proportions			
OCCUPATIONAL CLASS				
Professional	60%	26%	14%	90%
Managerial	62%	16%	8%	87%
Sales, Clerical	60%	18%	3%	90%
Service Workers	57%	20%	10%	90%
Craftsmen	53%	18%	5%	90%
Operatives	48%	13%	4%	76%
Laborers	48%	11%	2%	88%

Note: Adjusted proportions derived through multiple classification analysis. Proportions adjusted to compensate for variations across groups in age, sex, education, income, ethnic composition, and other background characteristics.

SOURCE: National Endowment for the Arts and U.S. Bureau of the Census, 1985 Survey of Public Participation in the Arts. MCA analysis results derived from: Robinson, John P., et al., *Public Participation in the Arts: Final Report on the 1985 Survey*, College Park, MD: University of Maryland Survey Research Center, December 1986, Tables 3.3, 3.4, 5.3a & b, and 5.4a & b.

her educational attainment and income level. Thus, much of the variation in reading habits across occupational classes could be attributed to these factors, rather than to occupation per se. When education, income, and other background factors were taken into account, the differences among occupational classes were considerably reduced. Some significant variation remained, though. The adjusted odds were about six-to-four in favor of a person having read literature if he or she were a professional, manager, or clerical employee, whereas they were slightly less than 50-50 if the person were an operative (such as a truck driver) or a laborer.

Marital Status

At first glance, there seemed to be only a weak and somewhat inconsistent relationship between a person's marital situation and his or her literature reading habits. Marital categories that contained a predominance of younger persons, namely the never married and separated, were slightly higher in literary participation, whereas the widowed, a group comprising mostly older persons, showed relatively low rates of reading and writing. The observed differences, however, appeared to be more a matter of age and education than of nuptial status. (Table 17.) After controlling for age, education, and race, a small but interesting difference emerged: people who were separated (but not those who were divorced) had slightly higher rates of literature reading, poetry reading, and creative writing, than people in the other marital categories. These findings suggest that people tend to turn to literature to help deal with the personal crisis of marital separation.

Presence of Children

Taking care of children can be time consuming. Time use surveys have shown that parents of young children, especially mothers, spend less time in eating, sleeping, and non-child-related recreational activities than adults without children.[49] In the 1985 SPPA data, however, there seemed to be little difference between the literature reading habits of adults with children and those of adults without children. After controlling for education, age, and other demographic factors, a small but significant difference did emerge, with parents of children under 6 years of age showing slightly lower

TABLE 17. Relationship Between Marital Status and Literature Reading, Poetry Reading, Creative Writing, and Book or Magazine Reading in Last 12 Months, U.S. Adults Aged 18 and Over, 1985.

| | Proportion of Population Group Who... | | | |
	Read Literature	Read Poetry	Did Creative Writing	Read Books, Magazines
ALL ADULTS	56%	19%	6%	86%
	Observed Proportions			
MARITAL STATUS				
Never Married	57%	22%	11%	86%
Married	56%	18%	5%	87%
Separated	55%	27%	10%	84%
Divorced	57%	13%	6%	87%
Widowed	49%	15%	0%	80%
	Adjusted Proportions			
MARITAL STATUS				
Never Married	55%	19%	9%	83%
Married	56%	19%	6%	86%
Separated	60%	29%	10%	89%
Divorced	56%	14%	6%	89%
Widowed	57%	19%	4%	87%

Note: Adjusted proportions derived through multiple classification analysis. Proportions adjusted to compensate for variations across groups in age, sex, education, income, ethnic composition, and other background characteristics.

SOURCE: National Endowment for the Arts, and U.S. Bureau of the Census, 1985 Survey of Public Participation in the Arts. MCA analysis results derived from: Robinson, John P., et al., *Public Participation in the Arts: Final Report on the 1985 Survey*, College Park, MD: University of Maryland Survey Research Center, December 1986, Tables 3.3, 3.4, 5.3a & b, and 5.4a & b.

TABLE 18. Relationship Between Parental Status and Literature Reading, Poetry Reading, Creative Writing, and Book or Magazine Reading in Last 12 Months, U.S. Adults Aged 18 and Over, 1985.

	Proportion of Population Group Who...			
	Read Literature	Read Poetry	Did Creative Writing	Read Books, Magazines
ALL ADULTS	56%	19%	6%	86%
PRESENCE AND AGE OF CHILDREN	Observed Proportions			
No children at home	56%	19%	6%	85%
One child under 6	53%	15%	7%	90%
Two children under 6	54%	18%	5%	87%
One child 6-11	57%	17%	8%	84%
Two children 6-11	61%	20%	9%	92%
PRESENCE AND AGE OF CHILDREN	Adjusted Proportions			
No children at home	57%	20%	6%	85%
One child under 6	50%	13%	5%	88%
Two children under 6	51%	18%	5%	83%
One child 6-11	55%	17%	8%	84%
Two children 6-11	57%	19%	10%	89%

Note: Adjusted proportions derived through multiple classification analysis. Proportions adjusted to compensate for variations across groups in age, sex, education, income, ethnic composition, and other background characteristics. For simplicity, groups with older children have been omitted.

SOURCE: National Endowment for the Arts and U.S. Bureau of the Census, 1985 Survey of Public Participation in the Arts. MCA analysis results derived from: Robinson, John P., et al., *Public Participation in the Arts: Final Report on the 1985 Survey*, College Park, MD: University of Maryland Survey Research Center, December 1986, Tables 3.3, 3.4, 5.3a & b, and 5.4a & b.

rates of literature and poetry reading than parents of children 6 and older, or non-parents. (Table 18.) The differences might have been greater if the survey had measured the number of books read, rather than just the fact of having read literature or not. Of course, for some adults, having children serves to bring them back into contact with literature or to increase their reading, at least of children's and youth-oriented books. In the BISG survey of book reading, more than a quarter of all adult fiction readers—or 10 percent of all adults—had read a juvenile or children's book in the last six months. Presumably much of this was parents reading to young children or reading aloud with older children. Reading to a child was also the third leading reason (after reading for pleasure and general knowledge) that fiction readers gave for reading. This reason was cited by 29 percent of the fiction readers.[50]

The Role of Television

Television watching is often cited as an activity that competes with reading and as a major reason why people do not read more literature. Yet television can be a spur to purchasing books and reading, as when an author appears on a talk show, a book is made into a television program or movie, or is advertised on television or mentioned or reviewed on a cultural program. In the BISG survey on book reading, respondents were asked to rate the importance of various factors in selecting books to read and purchase. "Seeing a movie or TV show based on the book" was among the top eight reasons for selecting a book, rated as "very important" by more than a quarter of the readers, and at least "somewhat important" by 60 percent of them.[51]

Adults interviewed in the SPPA were asked to report the number of hours they watched television on an average day. In the 1985 survey, close to 30 percent of all respondents reported that they watched 4 or more hours per day, which is here categorized as a "heavy" viewing pattern. About a quarter said they watched less than 2 hours per day ("light" viewing). The remainder, about 45 percent, watched between 2 and 4 hours ("moderate" viewing). A similar viewing breakdown was obtained in the 1982 SPPA. (Table 19.)

TABLE 19. Amounts of Daily Television Viewing Reported by U.S. Adults Aged 18 and Over, 1982 and 1985.

	Percent Distribution		Estimated Number of Viewers in Population	
	1985	1982	1985	1982
TELEVISION VIEWING				
Light (<2 Hrs/Day)	25.6%	24.0%	43.5 mil.	39.3 mil.
Moderate (2-3 Hrs)	45.9%	44.8%	78.1	73.3
Heavy (4 Hrs plus)	28.5%	31.2%	48.5	51.1
Total	100.0%	100.0%	170.1 mil.	163.7 mil.

SOURCE: National Endowment for the Arts and U.S. Bureau of the Census, 1982 and 1985 Surveys of Public Participation in the Arts, tabulations by N. Zill and M. Winglee from public use data files.

TABLE 20. Relationship Between Television Viewing and Literature Reading, Poetry Reading, Creative Writing, and Book or Magazine Reading in Last 12 Months, U.S. Adults Aged 18 and Over, 1982 and 1985.

	Proportion of Population Group Who...			
	Read Literature	Read Poetry	Did Creative Writing	Read Books, Magazines
	1982 Data			
ALL ADULTS	56.4%	19.8%	6.5%	84.1%
TELEVISION VIEWING				
Light (<2 Hrs/Day)	61.9%	28.8%	9.5%	81.2%
Moderate (2-3 Hrs)	58.8%	21.1%	6.7%	86.5%
Heavy (4 Hrs plus)	49.9%	14.6%	4.8%	79.3%
	1985 Data			
ALL ADULTS	56.0%			
TELEVISION VIEWING				
Light (<2 Hrs/Day)	59.6%			
Moderate (2-3 Hrs)	56.4%	n.a.	n.a.	n.a.
Heavy (4 Hrs plus)	52.9%			

SOURCE: National Endowment for the Arts and U.S. Bureau of the Census, 1982 and 1985 Surveys of Public Participation in the Arts, tabulations by N. Zill and M. Winglee from public use data files.

When the reports of TV watching were cross-tabulated with reports of literature reading, a negative but relatively weak relationship between reading and viewing emerged. In the 1985 data, the odds that "light" TV viewers had read a work of literature in the last 12 months were slightly better than average, about six-to-four. For "heavy" viewers, on the other hand, the odds were slightly below average, about 50-50. "Moderate" television viewers were about average in their literature reading propensity.

A similar but slightly stronger relationship was obtained with the 1982 survey data. (Table 20.) These data also permitted an analysis of the association between TV viewing and the other literary participation measures, which was not possible with the 1985 survey. Both poetry reading and creative writing showed negative relationships with time watching television, with the relationship for poetry being slightly stronger. Light TV viewers were twice as likely to have read poetry or done some creative writing as heavy viewers. Interestingly, the relationship between TV viewing and the reading of books and magazines was curvilinear, with the moderate viewing group showing a slightly higher proportion of readers than either the light or heavy viewing groups. This could be because poorly educated non-readers are apt to be either heavy viewers of television or non-viewers.

Countervailing tendencies. It may be that the overall association between TV viewing and literature reading is not stronger because there are opposing tendencies at work. As noted earlier, those who are active in one type of leisure activity tend to be active in other types as well. Some people simply do more than others, even though everyone is constrained by the number of hours in the day. This phenomenon is recognized in the saying, "If you want something done, ask the busy person to do it." We also know that there are large individual differences in reading speed. Moreover, time-use studies tell us that television watching is often done as a secondary activity; i.e., something that goes on while other activities are occurring.[52]

At some level, however, there must be a trade-off between one form of media participation and other forms. It seems likely that the trade-off between television and literature reading would be more visible if additional information about the types and quantity of reading done were available in the survey, or if the television viewers were further subdivided, into selective and non-selective viewers, for example.

Chapter 4
Expanding the Audience: What Can Be Done?

The State of Literature Reading

The survey results reported here contain both good and bad news for those who would like to see literature in America not only survive but flourish. The major piece of good news is that despite concerns about illiteracy and aliteracy in the United States, more than half of all American adults report that they have read some fiction, poetry, or drama within the last year. Levels of reading in the U.S. seem to be comparable to those in Great Britain and, as far as can be determined, other industrialized countries. In addition, general education levels have risen, recent generations of adults are more likely than older generations to have been encouraged to read as children, and growing numbers of people have been exposed to creative writing classes.

The surveys indicate that older adults are less likely to be readers of literature than middle-aged or young adults. However, the differences in reading propensities appear to be more a function of older citizens' lower education levels than of age per se, implying that literature reading levels among the elderly should go up in the future as the current cohorts of elders are replaced by the more educated senior citizens of tomorrow.

Other aspects of the survey results are less heartening. Follow-up questions asking what people meant when they said they had read novels or short stories revealed that some of the reports were erroneous and most involved the reading of lightweight, genre fiction (thrillers, romances, science fiction, horror stories, etc.) as opposed to more significant and enduring works. Of the 56 percent of adults who reported reading fiction, poetry, or drama within a 12-month period, less than half had read works of literary merit, comprising between a tenth and a quarter of the adult population. Moreover, the audience for meritorious contemporary works appeared to be smaller still, constituting something like 7 to 12 percent of all adults. Thus, although most Americans can and do read, followers of serious literature are distinctly in the minority.

Another discouraging finding is that while literature reading is likely to increase among older Americans, it seems to be decreasing among young adults. Data from several surveys point to a decline during the 1970s and 1980s in the frequency of reading among those under the age of 30. Literature has also become an art that is neglected by men and dominated by women. As of the mid-1980s, women made up nearly 60 percent of the readers, and almost two-thirds of the would-be writers of literature.

Whereas women are overrepresented, ethnic minorities continue to be underrepresented in the audience for literature. Despite the growing visibility and influence of Black and Hispanic writers, less than 45 percent of Black or Hispanic adults reported reading fiction, poetry, or drama. Their lower reading rates are largely attributable to their lower average education levels. But even when they have equivalent years of schooling, national testing programs have found that Black and Hispanic youths are less adept readers than non-minority young people. Blacks and Hispanic adults have had less exposure to creative writing classes than white adults, and, as children, Hispanics were less apt to have been encouraged to read by their parents.

The survey finding that may be most disappointing, however, is the simple fact that large numbers of American adults—44 percent—do not read literature at all. Most of the non-readers of literature know how to read. They have completed high school and been exposed to at least some instruction in literature appreciation. Yet they read nothing in the way of fiction, poetry, or drama. Why is it that literature in general and quality literature in particular are not read more widely? What can be done to encourage such reading?

Why Quality Literature Is Not Read More Widely

Three broad explanations can be suggested for why literature of merit is not read more widely: a shortage of readers who appreciate good literature, a dearth of writers who can communicate to a mass audience while maintaining high literary standards, and a need for more resources and knowledge to be applied to the promotion of literary works. Much attention has been paid of late to developments relevant to the first category; i.e., to changes in our educational system and broader society that may be producing fewer citizens who appreciate good literature and fine art. These developments are of legitimate concern to all who value the arts and humanities. When it comes to recommending steps to increase the audience for literature, however, the suggestions that seem most feasible to carry out fall mainly in the third category.

Readers Who Don't Appreciate

Is American society turning out fewer adults nowadays who have the skills and inclination to appreciate serious literature? Commentators on the U.S. cultural scene have pointed to a number of social trends that may be having stultifying effects on the enjoyment of literature, and on the appreciation of other arts and humanities as well.

Educational deterioration. Many critics claim that the U.S. educational system has deteriorated, and that high schools and colleges are doing a poor job of transmitting the Western cultural heritage to students. The schools have been accused of not teaching the skills required to appreciate great literature and art, not giving students a solid grounding in the classics, not nurturing a love for language, not requiring memorization of great poetry and prose, allowing students to get away with careless writing, and other fail-ings.[53] Research findings lend some support to these criticisms, but the picture is more complex than usually portrayed.

As is now well known, the College Entrance Examination Board's Scholastic Aptitude Tests and other nationwide testing pro-grams gave evidence of significant deterioration in student knowl-edge and proficiency during the late 1960s and 1970s. Not only did average test scores go down but also fewer students displayed high levels of achievement in either verbal or quantitative skills. Test scores have recovered somewhat during the 1980s, but the achievement levels of today's college-bound students are still sig-nificantly lower than those of comparable students in the early 1960s.[54]

The National Assessment of Educational Progress (NAEP) has found that today's high school students know relatively little about modern American literature, even though most have received in-struction in literature appreciation.[55] Earlier assessments showed that student attitudes about reading literature become progressively more negative as one goes from elementary school to junior high to high school students.[56] In 1985, NAEP assessed the literacy skills of young adults (ages 21-25) and found that 95 percent could read and understand the printed word, but only a small percentage could understand complex material. For example, only 9 percent of the young adults could understand an unfamiliar and rather subtle short poem by Emily Dickinson well enough to explain what the poet was trying to express.[57]

There is other research evidence, however, that casts litera-ture instruction in U.S. schools in a more favorable light. For one thing, U.S. schools are now at least *trying* to educate minority stu-dents who were written off in the past and are still relatively neglect-ed by educational systems in other nations. NAEP and other testing programs have shown that significant progress has been made during the last two decades in raising the basic reading and writing skills of Black and Hispanic students.[58] In an international comparison of literature education in ten countries, Alan Purves and his col-leagues found that "The United States brings a higher proportion of its age cohort farther along in reading than any other country in the sample without the best students suffering."[59] Overall, U.S.

students did not fare badly in international tests of literature achievement, although their achievement was not quite as good as that of British students in some areas and the U.S. students displayed more negative attitudes toward literature than students in other countries. Analyses of the international test results showed that home background was at least as important as school factors in accounting for individual differences in literature achievement. The analyses also called into question some of the prescriptions that have been made for improving literature instruction. It was found, for example, that students who did not frequently have to recite literature from memory performed better than those who did.[60]

Evidence from the College Board Achievement Testing Program indicates that the study of literature may be growing more popular, and U.S. high schools seem to be holding their own in teaching literature appreciation to the best students. The number of students who took the Literature Achievement Test increased by nearly 50 percent between 1980-1981 and 1985-1986 (going from 15,556 to 22,955 students), and the mean score on the test increased slightly (from 516 to 524) over the same interval.* However, only a small and rather select fraction of college bound students take the Literature Test. (In 1985-1986 there were more than 1.6 million who took the Scholastic Aptitude Test, 191 thousand, the English Composition Test, and more than 40 thousand, the American History Test.)[61]

Technological change and cultural decay. In contrast to those who blame our educational system for failing to maintain interest in literature, other observers point to profound cultural and technological changes that have occurred in our society and say it is unfair to expect the schools to overcome the negative effects of these developments.[62] Among the trends that may be working to the detriment of literature appreciation are:

- the increased availability of alternative forms of entertainment, not only television and movies, but also newspapers with a variety of feature articles, specialty magazines, electronic games and personal computers, music videos, etc.;

---

*Changes in test composition make it inadvisable to compare mean scores from the 1980s with those from Literature Achievement Tests given in earlier years.

- the explosion of scientific and technical knowledge, which has caused jargon to proliferate and compels the citizen who wants to be reasonably well-informed to spend more time reading factual material rather than literature;

- the breakdown of generally-accepted standards of artistic quality and taste in the face of challenges by avant-garde writers and artists, civil libertarians, ethnic minorities, feminists, and others;[63]

- the emergence of a youth-oriented entertainment industry that is blatantly vulgar and anti-intellectual, and that produces and promotes rock music, movies, and television shows aimed explicitly at the teenage and young adult audience;[64]

- the advent of a so-called "lite era," in which the mass media and commercial advertising have trained viewers and readers of all ages to be impatient with any work that requires serious and sustained attention.

Although it certainly seems plausible that some or all of these developments could have an effect on the reading and appreciation of literature, there has been no systematic research demonstrating connections between these trends and changes in literary participation.

The influence of television. Aside from the deterioration of the educational system, the emergence of television as the dominant medium of U.S. mass communication is most often cited as having a degrading influence on American civilization. Television programming has been described as addictive fare that is designed primarily to keep viewers watching through the commercials, thus taking up time that might otherwise be spent in reading or other more constructive pursuits. Television has also been accused of satiating the public appetite for narrative with "empty calories" instead of intellectual substance, of reducing public taste to the lowest common denominator, and of failing to challenge, inspire, or enlighten the viewer. It could be argued as well that television has lured writers who might produce works of broad and enduring appeal away from serious writing and into more lucrative but ephemeral projects, such as scripts for soap operas, situation comedies, and made-for-TV movies.

Only a weak negative association was found in the SPPA data between television viewing and literature reading, but there is little doubt that the advent of television has had profound effects on our cultural life.[65] Again, however, research that convincingly demonstrates links between television and trends in literary participation remains to be done.

Writers Who Don't Communicate

Some have argued that at least part of the blame for the relatively small audiences that contemporary literature and art command must be laid at the feet of the writers and artists themselves. The popular appeal of literature and the other arts has certainly been affected by the separation of the serious writer, painter, or composer from any sort of integral role in the operation or ceremonial life of the society.

Just how far artistic alienation has come is illustrated by a recent incident in which the late Robert Penn Warren, who was then serving as poet laureate of the United States, expressed indignation at the suggestion that he might produce a poem or two on national or patriotic themes during his tenure as laureate.[66] Instead of feeling honored that he was being called on to be the poetic voice of the nation, he apparently felt affronted by the notion. Warren is certainly not alone in rejecting the role of people's spokesman. Many contemporary writers and artists feel no obligation to deal with themes that might be of concern and interest to large numbers of their fellow citizens, or to make their work understandable, let alone entertaining, to any but the cognoscenti. It is scarcely surprising then, that the public chooses to stay away in droves from the work of these writers and artists.

The current situation was eloquently summarized by publisher Dan Lacy in a 1980 talk at the Center for the Book in the Library of Congress. Lacy observed that:

> The achievement of that communion between author and reader, artist and viewer, composer and audience by which creation is consummated depends on the possession of a common vocabulary of words and forms and structures

of meaning. Over the years this common coin grows worn with use so that the freshness and force of communication is blurred and dimmed. Young writers and painters and composers yearn to shatter them for new forms that, they feel, will better express their meaning. Better express indeed, but not better convey that meaning if the new-minted forms are not part of the audience's currency. Communion fails, full creation is aborted, and the artist's work in whatever field becomes a solipsism, to which he retreats with a greater willingness because of his growing contempt for and alienation from society.

One senses today how few are the artists in any field, at any adequate level of competence, who feel the strong central currents of society surge through them to shape their work—in the sense that Shakespeare and Haydn and da Vinci felt at one with their times. In another day even those creators and thinkers who felt most alienated and hostile to the dominant forces of their times—such as Karl Marx, Zola, or Brecht—yet felt society itself important— quite literally terribly important—and themselves and their work important in challenging it. They were therefore called forth to their utmost not only to express but to convey their meanings, to reach minds, to engage themselves to the fullest with the life of their time—whether as its voice or its foe. I do not find it so today.[67]

Publishers Who Don't Promote

In addition to the large-scale social changes described above, there are more mundane reasons why contemporary literature is not more widely read. These reasons have to do with a lack of resources devoted to the promotion of literary books and deficiencies in their packaging, advertising, and distribution. In these areas, there are actions available to private firms and public organizations that might help to boost the sales and readership of contemporary works of merit.

As things now stand, relatively little money or effort is spent on publishing literary books, especially in comparison to the large amounts spent promoting television programs, movies, popular magazines, and other mass media products that compete with books for the reader's attention. The modest resources that are invested in promotion tend to be spent in standard ways: sending the author on a book tour, distributing free copies to reviewers and prominent individuals who might provide testimonials, placing advertisements in literary magazines or the book review sections of newspapers, etc. Most of these methods consist largely of preaching to the converted rather than trying to make new disciples from among those who read only popular fiction, those who do not read literature at all, or those from ethnic minorities and other social groups who are underrepresented in the literary audience.

There is, to be sure, a good commercial reason why more promotion is not done: the money to support it is not there. As mentioned earlier, most volumes of serious fiction, poetry, and drama do not sell many copies, even if they have received excellent reviews. Publishing these works is typically a losing or marginally profitable proposition. More promotion might lead to more sales, but in most cases the risks involved seem to be too great or the projected sales too small to warrant the investment of additional resources. Efforts to publicize literary works more widely could, of course, be subsidized by the profits (if any) that publishers make on their more successful books, or through promotional campaigns conducted by libraries and booksellers, by cash and in-kind contributions from corporations, and by grants from private foundations or public agencies.* All of these forms of subsidy are now customary in the performing arts, and there seems little reason why they should not be applied more widely to the art of literature. In addition to the need for more resources devoted to promotion, however, promotional efforts should be better informed by knowledge about why people read and how they go about selecting the particular books they do.

Applying Research to Encourage Literature Reading

A number of steps could be taken to apply research findings to the process of disseminating information about new and classic

---

*The NEA's Literature Program does provide a small amount of support, on an annual basis through matching grants, for "audience development projects". These include literary promotion projects, small press bookfairs, radio programs, etc.

books. Illustrative suggestions are offered in the following paragraphs.

Paying attention to subject matter. One research result that has received insufficient attention from those who sell and lend books is that one of the main reasons people choose to read the books they do is because they are interested in the subject matter dealt with in the books and are seeking to expand their general information about the time, place, people, or events in question.[68] This finding applies to the reading of both fiction and non-fiction. Yet most bookstores and libraries are organized as if the reasons for reading fiction were entirely separate and distinct from those for reading non-fiction. Fiction and non-fiction works are kept in different areas and there is no easy way for someone who is interested in, say, browsing through novels about the U.S. Civil War to do so. A display or shelving system that brought together fiction and non-fiction books on given topics might well tempt the person who is interested in a subject, but who does not ordinarily read fiction, to buy or borrow a novel that deals with the subject. Likewise, in advertising a new work of fiction that deals with a given subject or period, publishers could make use of special interest periodicals and mailing lists that would reach those with a proven interest in the subject or period. At present, this is rarely done.

Guiding readers to books they are likely to enjoy. Book research has shown that fiction readers could use more information to help guide their selection of books to read. For example, a study by Nicholas Spenceley and Peter Mann found that it was not uncommon for library patrons to borrow a novel just because it looked interesting on the shelf, without prior knowledge of the author or title. When they did this, however, they wound up having a positive reaction to the book only 40 percent of the time.[69] This was well below the satisfaction levels of readers who had more specific information about the title or author prior to borrowing a book. This suggests that in order to increase the chances of reader satisfaction, which would, in turn, lead to more reading of contemporary literature, librarians, publishers, and literature programs should be providing potential readers with more guidance of the following sort: "If you enjoyed (Book A), you're likely to enjoy (Books B, C, and D)." Moreover, it would be preferable if this guidance were based on actual surveys of reader satisfaction, rather than on the judgment of individual experts or the desires of publishers to plug particular titles in their catalogs.

Getting genre fans to read quality fiction. It would appear that more could be done to encourage the readers of genre fiction to explore more serious literary works. One way of doing this is to establish, through research, which works of quality literature are apt to appeal to readers of a particular genre, and then to publicize those works through advertisements and outlets that are likely to reach the genre readers. Other steps that might be taken are to give public recognition to those writers of thrillers, romances, science fiction, etc., whose novels or short stories evince superior literary qualities, and to encourage good writers who are not widely read to attempt some genre or genre-like writing in order to build a bigger following for their work.

Using newspapers to reach non-readers of literature. Surveys show that one way to reach people who read but do not read literature is through newspapers and news magazines, suggesting that more should be done to publicize new books and promote literature reading in general through newspapers.* Books could also be advertised more extensively in newspapers, and not just in the book review sections. As is done for the performing arts, newspapers might be persuaded to run a regular literary "billboard" that combined small advertisements for a number of different books in one section, with the advertising space being sold at reduced rates. Literature programs could also encourage newspapers to run more feature articles about books and authors, to bring back the serialization of quality fiction in their pages, and to print more poems, particularly ones that are relatively accessible to readers who have not been steeped in Ezra Pound and Wallace Stevens.

Employing television more effectively. Increasing the amount of television publicity for serious literature does not mean simply getting more authors on talk shows, for authors' appearances do not always enhance book sales. Valuable principles can be learned, though, from programs that have been successful at encourag-

---

*One attempt to do this is the PEN Syndicated Fiction Project, which has placed short stories in major newspapers across the country since 1978.

ing reading and stimulating book sales. These include the children's reading series *Cover to Cover* and *Reading Rainbow,* and the adult-oriented book review program, *Bookmark.* Among the lessons these shows teach are to select the books to be featured carefully, choosing ones that have both high quality and wide appeal, to present excerpts from the books' stories on the show, with illustrations or dramatizations that help to involve the viewer, and to ensure that the viewer can obtain the books without great difficulty. (The last point includes making certain that the book is still in print.)

Supporting promising developments in book marketing. Literature support programs should also be making efforts to identify, encourage, and disseminate information about promising innovations in the marketing and distribution of literary books. Two recent examples of developments that may make a difference in the sales and readership of today's literature are the proliferation of book discussion groups and the emergence of the trade paperback series.

Book discussion groups are small gatherings of adults who assign themselves a series of common readings and get together regularly to discuss the books and socialize. These groups, which have apparently become fairly popular in a number of metropolitan areas, are a perfect mechanism for expanding the range of people who read modern literature as well as the number of books read. Libraries and publishers could help to suggest and supply reading matter for these groups and stimulate the formation of more such groups.

Trade paperback series, such as Vintage Contemporaries, Scribners Signature Editions, and Penguin Contemporary American Fiction, are a group of original or reprinted novels by different contemporary authors that are published in higher–priced paperbound editions with an imprint name and a uniform cover format. Books in the series also appear together in special bookstore displays, and these displays are often prominently exhibited in both local literary bookstores and in chain stores. Novels published in these series have sold 10-to-20 times as many copies as the typical literary novel that comes out in an individual hard-cover edition. Although some critics have qualms about books being bought and sold by "brand name" rather than on their individual merits, this marketing innovation seems to have given a number of serious authors a substantial boost in readership.[70]

Promoting both established and developing authors. It might seem logical to focus publicity efforts for contemporary literature on authors whose works have artistic distinction but little hope of commercial success. Promotional efforts for writers like John Barth, Joan Didion, Joseph Heller, Anne Tyler, John Updike, Gore Vidal, or Tom Wolfe seem unnecessary because their names are widely known in literary circles and their books usually sell quite well in comparison with most works of serious fiction. Yet, if the goal is to expand the audience for contemporary literature beyond its current bounds, promoting established as well as struggling authors might well be in order. It is likely that the aforementioned writers and their works are not familiar to most members of the public at large, as demonstrated by the 1984 poll showing that most Americans did not recognize the name George Orwell. Moreover, the number of people who buy or borrow even a best-selling book by one of these authors is small in comparison with the number of college-educated adults in the U.S. or the number of people who watch a prime-time television show. Thus, the notion of including such prominent authors in literature promotion campaigns is far from ridiculous. Indeed, their inclusion would seem to be a sensible way to get more people reading quality literature.

* * *

In conclusion, it seems possible that the readership of contemporary fiction, poetry, and drama could be greatly increased if more private and public resources were devoted to the encouragement of literature reading and if promotional efforts made better use of research knowledge about why people read and how they select the books that they do. Ways in which research findings could be applied include paying more attention to the importance of subject matter in people's selections of books to read, providing potential buyers and borrowers with guidance about books they are likely to enjoy, encouraging fans of genre fiction to explore more serious literary works, using newspapers to reach a wide array of readers (including those who do not currently read literature), employing television more effectively to promote books, supporting such promising new developments as book discussion groups and trade paperback series, and promoting works by established as well as developing authors.

The actions suggested above will not work wonders. In the long run, the viability and reach of the literary enterprise depends less on marketing techniques than on how well our society can cultivate readers with the skills and sensibilities to appreciate great literature and writers with the craft and imagination to entertain, challenge, and enlighten large numbers of their compatriots. Given the current situation, however, with many potential readers in the population but few reading serious works on any but an occasional basis, it does seem that increased investment in promotional efforts would produce a notable and much needed expansion in the audience for literature.

TECHNICAL APPENDIX

How well can we predict whether a person will be a literature reader, knowing basic facts about him or her such as age, sex, race, education, income, and place of residence? The statistical method used to answer this question was logistic regression analysis.[1] Like linear discriminant analysis, logistic regression finds a weighted combination of characteristics that best accounts for the observed distribution of people into two mutually exclusive classes (in this case, readers and non-readers). Unlike linear models, however, logistic regression fits the data to a curve or, in multiple dimensions, a curved solid, rather than a straight line or rectilinear solid.[2]

Specifically, let the dependent variable, Y, be equal to one if the person is a reader, and zero if he or she is not. Then the probability, p_i, that the ith individual is a reader, is represented by the equation:

$$p_i = 1/\{1 + e^{[-\alpha - \Sigma_j(X_{ij} * \beta_j)]}\}$$

where e is the base of the natural logarithms, alpha is the intercept term, and β_j is the regression weight for the jth predictor variable. The optimal values of the α and β weights are derived using the modified Gauss-Newton method of maximum-likelihood estimation. (The LOGIST computer program in the SAS statistical software package was used to develop the models.)[3]

Logistic regression has several advantages over linear regression for predicting dichotomous outcomes like literature reading. First, the logistic model is inherently interactive in its depiction of the relationships among the predictor and criterion variable and, as such, is probably closer to the underlying reality than is the simple additive model of linear regression.[4] Second, it is often more difficult to achieve an increase in the probability of occurrence of an outcome at the extremes of its probability distribution (i.e., when the probability is very low or very high). The logistic model is able to accomodate such "floor and ceiling" effects. Linear regression, by contrast, assumes that a unit change in the value of the predictor variable will produce a constant level of change regardless of where one is on the probability distribution of the dependent variable.[5]

Third, logistic regression always yields predicted probabilities between 0 and 1. Linear regression, on the other hand, can produce predicted values beyond 0 and 1, in effect predicting probabilities below zero and in excess of 100 percent. Finally, the logistic model makes fewer assumptions about the underlying distributions of variables (e.g., no multivariate normality assumption for covariates). When distributional assumptions are violated, logistic regression still yields unbiased estimates of the standard errors of coefficients, whereas ordinary least squares regression may not.

Appendix Table I summarizes the results of multiple logistic regressions performed on data from the 1982 and 1985 Survey of Public Participation in the Arts. The dependent variable was whether or not the respondent reported reading literature during the previous twelve months. The independent variables were the respondent's age (in single years), sex (coded "1" if female, "0" if male), race (coded "1" if black, "0" if non-black), educational attainment (years of regular school completed), income (total dollars, broken down into 14 categories), central city residence (coded "1" if the respondent lived in the central city of a metropolitan area, "0" otherwise), and non-metropolitan residence (coded "1" if the respondent lived outside any metropolitan area, "0" if inside the suburbs or central city of a metropolitan area). Independent models were developed for the 1982 and 1985 surveys.

The top panel of the table shows the contribution of each demographic characteristic to the prediction of literature reading. The middle panel gives the computed regression coefficients and their standard errors. The bottom panel presents several measures of the predictive accuracy of the model.

A chi-square test was performed to assess whether the logistic-regression model gave a discernibly better prediction than a model based on the presumption of no association between the predictors and the criterion. A statistic called **R**, derived from the model chi-square, is one measure of the overall predictive ability of the model. The **R** statistic is similar to the multiple correlation coefficient in the normal setting, and incorporates a correction for the number of parameters being estimated.

Individual **r** statistics ("partial rs") were computed for each predictor variable. Ranging in value from -1 to $+1$, the partial **r** provides a measure of the contribution of each variable to the prediction, net of the effects of the other predictors. In the top panel of Appendix Table I, the independent variables are listed in rank order, based on the relative sizes of their partial correlation coefficients. Rank correlation coefficients showing the unadjusted relationship between each predictor and the criterion are presented for comparison.

Once the best-fitting logistic model has been determined, the observed cases can be classsified as readers or non-readers based on the model. A case is predicted to be 1 on the dependent variable if the estimated probability for that case is greater than a chosen value. The **proportion of cases correctly classified** is another measure of the predictive ability of the model presented in Table I, as are the **false positive rate** and the **false negative rate**. The former is the proportion of predicted positives (readers) who were actually negatives (non-readers). The latter is the proportion of predicted negatives (non-readers) who were actually positives (readers).

Because the predicted probabilities are continuous, the point at which they are divided into positives and negatives is somewhat arbitrary. An alternative way of assessing the predictive ability of the model, one which is independent of a specific cut-point, is to calculate an index of rank-order correlation between the predicted probabilities and the dependent variable. This measure is also shown for each model.

Appendix Table II summarizes the results of multiple-logistic regressions in which the dependent variable was whether the respondent had read poetry or attended a poetry reading during the previous 12 months, as reported in the 1982 and 1985 SPPA. The predictor variables were the same as those in Table I. Appendix Table III summarizes regression models in which the criterion was whether the respondent reported doing any creative writing during the previous 12 months, and the predictor variables were again the same.

Substantive conclusions derived from these regression analyses are described at appropriate points in the main text.

NOTES

1. S.H. Walker and D.B. Duncan, "Estimation of the Probability of an Event as a Function of Several Independent Variables," *Biometrika,* **54** (1967): 167-179.

2. S.J. Press and S. Wilson, "Choosing Between Logistic Regression and Discriminant Analysis," *Journal of the American Statistical Association,* **73** (1978): 699-705.

3. Frank E. Harrell, Jr., "The LOGIST Procedure," in *SUGI Supplemental Library User's Guide, 1983 Edition,* (Cary, North Carolina: SAS Institute, Inc., 1983), 181-202.

4. Alfred DeMaris, "Interpreting Logistic Regression Results: A Critical Commentary," *Journal of Marriage and the Family,* **52** (February 1990): 271-277.

5. S. Philip Morgan and Jay D. Teachman, "Logistic Regression: Description, Examples, and Comparisons," *Journal of Marriage and the Family,* **50** (November 1988): 929-936.

TABLES TO THE APPENDIX

TABLE I. Multiple Logistic Models Predicting Whether Adults Have Read Literature in Last Year, Based on their Demographic Characteristics (Age, Gender, Race, Education, Income, and Metropolitan Residence), U.S. Adults 18 and Over, 1982 and 1985.

			Contribution of Individual Predictors		
		1982		1985	
Variable	Rank	Obs. r	Adj. r	Rank	Adj. r
Education	1	.39	.27**	1	.26**
Gender	2	.14	.16**	2	.16**
Income	3	.20	.05**	3	.06**
Race	4	−.10	−.05**	4	−.05**
Age	5	−.11	−.02**	—	.00
Non-Metro Residence	6	−.07	−.01*	5	−.03*
Central City Residence	—	.00	.00	—	.00

			Regression Coefficients	
	1982		1985	
		Standard		Standard
Variable	Beta	Error	Beta	Error
Intercept	−2.48	.109	−2.33	.105
Education (years attained)	.13	.003	.12	.004
Gender (Male = 0, Female = 1)	.87	.037	.86	.041
Income	.05	.007	.04	.006
Race (Non-Black = 0, Black = 1)	−.45	.063	−.46	.069
Age (in years)	−.003	.001	.000	.001
Non-Metro Residence (= 1, else = 0)	−.09	.043	−.18	.049
Central City Residence (= 1, else = 0)	.02	.046	.003	.050

		Predictive Accuracy	
Index	1982		1985
Proportion of Cases Correctly Classified	69%		68%
False Positive Rate	26%		27%
False Negative Rate	37%		38%
Multiple Correlation Coefficient (R)	.38**		.36**
Rank Correlation Between Predicted Probability and Response	.49**		.48**
Number of Cases	15,667		12,361

** p < .01
 * p < .05
+p < .10

Obs. r = Observed correlation between predictor and criterion.

Adj. r = Partial correlation between predictor and criterion, net of effects of other predictors in model.

Source: N. Zill and M. Winglee, analysis of public use tapes from 1982 and 1985 Survey of Public Participation in the Arts, National Endowment for the Arts, and U.S. Bureau of the Census, 1987.

TABLE II. Multiple Logistic Models Predicting Whether Adults Have Read Poetry in Last Year, Based on their Demographic Characteristics (Age, Gender, Race, Education, Income, and Metropolitan Residence), U.S. Adults 18 and Over, 1982 and 1985.

	Contribution of Individual Predictors				
		1982		1985	
Variable	*Rank*	*Obs. r*	*Adj. r*	*Rank*	*Adj. r*
Education	1	.27	.24**	1	.18**
Gender	2	.08	.11**	2	.09**
Age	3	−.11	−.05**	—	.00
Non-Metro Residence	4	−.02	.03*	—	.00
Central City Residence	5	.01	.02+	—	.00
Income	6	.07	.02+	—	.00
Race	—	−.04	−.01	3	−.03+

	Regression Coefficients			
	1982		1985	
		Standard		*Standard*
Variable	*Beta*	*Error*	*Beta*	*Error*
Intercept	−3.02	.248	−2.89	.305
Education (years attained)	.11	.007	.08	.009
Gender (Male = 0, Female = 1)	.59	.088	.49	.115
Age (in years)	−.009	.003	−.001	.003
Non-Metro Residence (= 1, else = 0)	.21	.103	−.09	.137
Central City Residence (= 1, else = 0)	.18	.106	−.09	.139
Income	−.03	.015	.009	.017
Race (Non-Black = 0, Black = 1)	−.23	.156	−.41	.216

	Predictive Accuracy	
Index	1982	1985
Proportion of Cases Correctly Classified	76%	75%
False Positive Rate	68%	71%
False Negative Rate	13%	14%
Multiple Correlation Coefficient (R)	.29**	.21**
Rank Correlation Between Predicted Probability and Response	.41**	.32**
Number of Cases	3,849	2,132

** $p < .01$
* $p < .05$
+ $p < .10$

Obs. r = Observed correlation between predictor and criterion.

Adj. r = Partial correlation between predictor and criterion, net of effects of other predictors in model.

Source: N. Zill and M. Winglee, analysis of public use tapes from 1982 and 1985 Survey of Public Participation in the Arts, National Endowment for the Arts, and U.S. Bureau of the Census, 1987.

TABLE III. Multiple Logistic Models Predicting Whether Adults Have Done Creative Writing in Last Year, Based on their Demographic Characteristics (Age, Gender, Race, Education, Income, and Metropolitan Residence), U.S. Adults 18 and Over, 1982 and 1985.

| | Contribution of Individual Predictors | | | | |
| | 1982 | | | 1985 | |
Variable	Rank	Obs. r	Adj. r	Rank	Adj. r
Education	1	.17	.22**	1	.22**
Age	2	-.14	-.14**	2	-.12**
Gender	3	.06	.10**	4	.08**
Central City Residence	4	.04	.05*	—	.00
Income	5	.03	-.03+	—	.00
Non-Metro Residence	—	-.04	.00	3	-.09**
Race	—	-.01	.00	—	.00

| | Regression Coefficients | | | |
| | 1982 | | 1985 | |
Variable	Beta	Standard Error	Beta	Standard Error
Intercept	-3.54	.400	-3.93	.523
Education (years attained)	.12	.012	.12	.017
Age (in years)	-.03	.005	-.03	.007
Gender (Male = 0, Female = 1)	.65	.144	.55	.189
Central City Residence (= 1, else = 0)	.41	.164	-.03	.208
Income	-.05	.024	.003	.028
Non-Metro Residence (= 1, else = 0)	-.07	.179	-.84	.273
Race (Non-Black = 0, Black = 1)	-.30	.253	-.31	.346

| | Predictive Accuracy | |
Index	1982	1985
Proportion of Cases Correctly Classified	92%	92%
False Positive Rate	88%	87%
False Negative Rate	3%	3%
Multiple Correlation Coefficient (R)	.32**	.32**
Rank Correlation Between Predicted Probability and Response	.51**	.54**
Number of Cases	3,848	2,137

** p < .01
* p < .05
+ p < .10

Obs. r = Observed correlation between predictor and criterion.

Adj. r = Partial correlation between predictor and criterion, net of effects of other predictors in model.

Source: N. Zill and M. Winglee, analysis of public use tapes from 1982 and 1985 Survey of Public Participation in the Arts, National Endowment for the Arts, and U.S. Bureau of the Census, 1987.

Notes

1. Jonathan Yardley, "The Increasing Irrelevance of Writing," *The Washington Post* (Monday, December 8, 1986), D2. Idem, "Blanking Verse in the L.A. Times," *The Washington Post* (Monday, May 11, 1987), B2.

2. Allan Bloom, *The Closing of the American Mind* (New York: Simon and Schuster, 1987), 62.

3. E.D. Hirsch, Jr., *Cultural Literacy: What Every American Needs To Know* (Boston, Houghton Mifflin, 1987).

4. Nick Thimmesch, (Ed.), *Aliteracy: People Who Can Read But Won't* (Washington, DC: The American Enterprise Institute, 1984).

5. Martha S. Hill, "Patterns of Time Use," in: *Time, Goods, and Well-Being*, F. Thomas Juster and Frank P. Stafford, Eds. (Ann Arbor, MI: Institute for Social Research, University of Michigan, 1985), 138.

6. John P. Robinson, et al., *Americans' Participation in the Arts: A 1983-84 Arts-Related Trend Study, Final Report* (College Park, MD: University of Maryland Survey Research Center, 1986), 86-87.

7. National Assessment of Educational Progress, *Literature and U.S. History: The Instructional Experience and Factual Knowledge of High*

School Juniors, by A.N. Applebee, J.A. Langner, and Ina V.S. Mullis (Princeton, NJ: Educational Testing Service, October 1987), 10-13. See also: Lynne V. Cheney, *American Memory: A Report on the Humanities in the Nation's Public Schools,* National Endowment for the Humanities Report No. NEH-636 (Washington, DC: U.S. Government Printing Office, 1987). Diane Ravitch and Chester E. Finn, Jr., *What Do Our 17-Year Olds Know? A Report on the First National Assessment of History and Literature* (New York: Harper & Row, 1987).

8. U.S. Bureau of the Census, *Statistical Abstract of the United States: 1987 (107th edition),* Table No. 368, "Quantity of Books Sold and Value of U.S. Domestic Consumer Expenditures, by Type of Publication and Market Area: 1974 to 1985." (Washington, DC: U.S. Government Printing Office, 1986).

9. National Assessment of Educational Progress, *Literature and U.S. History.* Lynne V. Cheney, *American Memory: A Report on the Humanities in the Nation's Public Schools.* Diane Ravitch and Chester E. Finn, Jr., *What Do Our 17-Year Olds Know?*

10. J.P. Robinson, C.A. Keegan, T. Hanford, and T.A. Triplett, *Public Participation in the Arts: Final Report on the 1982 Survey,* prepared under Grant No. 12-4050-003 from the National Endowment for the Arts (College Park, MD: University of Maryland Survey Research Center, October 1985), Chapter 7. See also R.J. Orend, *Socialization And Participation in the Arts,* (National Endowment for the Arts, 1989).

11. National Assessment of Educational Progress, *Music 1971-79: Results from the Second National Music Assessment,* Report No. 10-Mu-01 (Denver, CO: Education Commission of the States, November 1981). Idem, *Art and Young Americans, 1974-79: Results from the Second National Art Assessment,* Report No. 10-A-01 (Denver, CO: Education Commission of the States, December 1981).

12. U.S. Bureau of the Census, *Statistical Abstract of the United States: 1987 (107th edition),* Table No. 370, "New Books and New Editions Published by Subject, 1970 to 1985, . . . ;" (Washington, DC: U.S. Government Printing Office, 1986).

13. John P. Dessauer, "U.S. Retail Book Sales by Subject: A First Estimate," *Book Research Quarterly,* Vol. 2, No. 4, Winter 1986-1987, 15-17.

14. U.S. Bureau of the Census, *Statistical Abstract of the United States: 1987 (107th edition),* Table No. 370, "New Books and New Editions Published by Subject, 1970 to 1985, . . .".

15. For methodology of the SPPA studies see Robinson et al., *Public Participation in the Arts: Final Report on the 1982 Survey.* John P. Robin-

son, Carol A. Keegan, Marcia Karth and Timothy A. Triplett, *Public Participation in the Arts: Final Report on the 1985 Survey* (College Park, MD: University of Maryland Survey Research Center, December 1986), Chapter 2 and Appendix A. For methodology of the ARTS survey see John P. Robinson et al., *Americans' Participation in the Arts: A 1983-84 Arts-Related Trend Study.* For methodology of the BISG study see Market Facts, Inc.and Research & Forecasts, Inc., *1983 Consumer Research Study on Reading and Book Purchasing. Vol.1: Focus on Adults* (New York: Book Industry Study Group, Inc., 1984), 219.

16. Peter Mann, *From Author to Reader: A Social Study of Books* (London: Routledge & Kegan Paul, 1982), 147.

17. See Robinson et al., *Final Report on the 1982 Survey, Final Report on the 1985 Survey.*

18. The 65-percent figure represents the projected number of readers of literature divided by the projected number of readers of books and magazines. When the two survey items were actually cross-tabulated against one another, a small percentage of respondents were found to have given inconsistent responses. That is, they said that they read literature in the previous 12 months, but did not read books or magazines. Thus, the proportion derived from cross-tabulation is slightly lower than the figure cited.

19. The BISG figures on fiction book readership (39 percent) and overall book readership (50 percent) were lower than the SPPA figure on literature readership (56 percent). This is probably because the BISG used a 6-month reference period, and the SPPA, a 12-month reference period. Also, the BISG questions referred only to books, whereas the SPPA question included fiction, poetry, and plays in magazines as well as in books. The BISG figure on overall readership (92 percent) was higher than the SPPA figure (86 percent), probably because the BISG question included newspapers, which were not mentioned by the SPPA.

20. Mann, *From Author to Reader: A Social Study of Books,* pp. 147-148. Idem, "The Novel in British Society," *Poetics,* Vol. 12, 435-448, 1983, 442).

21. Kay Gill and Donald P. Boyden, (Eds.), *Gale Directory of Publications, 120th Edition* (Detroit: Gale Research Company, 1988). *The Standard Periodical Directory, Tenth Edition* (New York: Oxbridge Communications, 1987). Yardley, "Blanking Verse in the L.A. Times."

22. Dessauer, "U.S. Retail Book Sales by Subject."

23. Market Facts, Inc., *1983 Consumer Research Study,* 1: 167-168.

24. Dessauer, "U.S. Retail Book Sales by Subject."

25. Market Facts, Inc., *1983 Consumer Research Study*, 1: 71.

26. Robinson et al., *Final Report on the 1982 Survey*, Chapter 3.

27. L.A. Wood, "Demographics of Mass Market Consumers," *Book Research Quarterly*, Vol. 3, No. 1, Spring 1987, 31-39.

28. Market Facts, Inc., *1983 Consumer Research Study*, 1: 64-68.

29. U.S. Bureau of the Census, *Statistical Abstract of the United States: 1987 (107th edition)*, Table No. 368, "Quantity of Books Sold and Value of U.S. Domestic Consumer Expenditures, by Type of Publication and Market Area: 1974 to 1985."

30. William S. Lofquist, "Book Publishing," U.S. Department of Commerce, *U.S. Industrial Outlook — 1988*, 1988, 29-9.

31. J.G. Bachman, L.D. Johnston, and P.M. O'Malley, *Monitoring the Future* (Ann Arbor, MI: University of Michigan, Institute for Social Research, annual volumes, 1975-1986). See also: "Daily Activity Patterns of High School Seniors," Select Committee on Children, Youth, and Families, U.S. House of Representatives, *U.S. Children and Their Families: Current Conditions and Recent Trends, 1989* (Washington, DC: U.S. Government Printing Office, September 1989); 226-227.

32. Lofquist, "Book Publishing," 29-7—29-11.

33. Robinson et al., *Americans' Participation in the Arts.*

34. Mann, "The Novel in British Society," 443.

35. Market Facts, Inc., *1983 Consumer Research Study*, 1: passim.

36. U.S. Bureau of the Census, Statistical Abstract of the United States: 1987 (107th edition), Table No. 368, "Quantity of Books Sold and Value of U.S. Domestic Consumer Expenditures, by Type of Publication and Market Area: 1974 to 1985;" and Table No. 376, "Selected Recreational Activities: 1970 to 1985."

37. Market Facts, Inc., *1983 Consumer Research Study*, 1: passim.

38. Eleanor E. Maccoby and Carol N. Jacklin, *The Psychology of Sex Differences* (Stanford, CA: Stanford University Press, 1974), 83-87. National Center for Health Statistics, K.W. Schaie and J. Roberts, "School Achievement of Children 6-11 Years, as Measured by the Reading and Arithmetic Subtests of the Wide Range Achievement Test, United States," *Vital and Health Statistics*, Series 11, No. 103, Public Health Service (Washington, DC: U.S. Government Printing Office, June 1970). Idem, "School Achievement of Children by Demographic and Socioeconomic Factors, United States," *Vital and Health Statistics*, Series 11, No. 109, DHEW Publication No. (HSM) 72-1011, Public Health Service

(Washington, DC: U.S. Government Printing Office, November 1971). National Center for Health Statistics, J. Roberts, "Intellectual Development of Children as Measured by the Wechsler Intelligence Scale for Children, United States," *Vital and Health Statistics,* Series 11, No. 107, DHEW Publication No. (HSM) 72-1004, Public Health Service (Washington, DC: U.S. Government Printing Office, August 1971). Idem, "Intellectual Development of Children by Demographic and Socioeconomic Factors, United States," *Vital and Health Statistics,* Series 11, No. 110, DHEW Publication No. (HSM) 72-1012, Public Health Service (Washington, DC: U.S. Government Printing Office, December 1971). National Center for Health Statistics, D.K. Vogt, "Literacy Among Youths 12-17 Years, United States," *Vital and Health Statistics,* Series 11, No. 131, DHEW Publication No. (HRA) 74-1613, Public Health Service (Washington, DC: U.S. Government Printing Office, December 1973). National Assessment of Educational Progress, "Males Dominate in Educational Success," *Spotlight: NAEP Newsletter,* Vol. VIII, No. 5, October 1975 (Denver, CO: Education Commission of the States). Alan Feingold, "Cognitive Gender Differences Are Disappearing," *American Psychologist,* Vol. 43, No. 2, February 1988, 95-103.

39. Nicholas Zill and James L. Peterson, "Learning to Do Things Without Help," in Luis M. Laosa & Irving E. Sigel (Eds.), *Families As Learning Environments for Children* (New York: Plenum Publishing, 1982), 343-374.

40. National Center for Health Statistics, D.C. Hitchcock and G.D. Pinder, "Reading and Arithmetic Achievement Among Youths 12-17 Years, as Measured by the Wide Range Achievement Test, United States," *Vital and Health Statistics,* Series 11, No. 136, DHEW Publication No. (HRA) 74-1618, Public Health Service (Washington, DC: U.S. Government Printing Office, February 1974).

41. L. Ramist and S. Arbeiter, *Profiles, College-Bound Seniors, 1985* (New York: College Entrance Examination Board, 1986), 12-13, 22-23, 102, and 14, 24.

42. de Beauvoir, Simone, *The Coming of Age,* (translation by Patrick O'Brian of *La Vieillesse*), (New York: G.P. Putnam's Sons, 1972), 398-404.

> "Writing is. . .a complex activity: it means a simultaneous preference for the imaginary and a desire to communicate...The project of writing therefore implies a tension between a refusal of the world in which men live and a certain appeal to men themselves: the writer is both for and against them. This is a difficult position: it implies very lively passions; and to be maintained for a considerable length of time it calls for strength.
> "Old age reduces strength; it deadens emotion. . .The ten-

sion born of the reconciliation of two projects that are if not contradictory then at least divergent, slackens. The elderly writer finds himself deprived of that quality which Flaubert called *alacrité*." (pp. 400-401)

43. Edward C. Bryant, Ezra Glaser, Morris H. Hansen, and Arthur Kirsch, *Associations Between Educational Outcomes and Background Variables: A Review of Selected Literature,* Contract Report by Westat, Inc., A Monograph of the National Assessment of Educational Progress (Denver, CO: Education Commission of the States, 1974).

44. National Assessment of Educational Progress, *The Reading Report Card, 1971-88: Trends from the Nation's Report Card,* by Ina V.S. Mullis and Lynn B. Jenkins, Report No. 19-R-01, (Princeton, NJ: Educational Testing Service, January 1990), 64.

45. Edward C. Bryant, Ezra Glaser, Morris H. Hansen, and Arthur Kirsch, *Associations Between Educational Outcomes and Background Variables: A Review of Selected Literature.* Alison Clarke-Stewart, *Child Care in the Family: A Review of Research and Some Propositions for Policy* (New York: Academic Press, 1977). Lee Willerman, "Effects of Families on Intellectual Development," *American Psychologist,* Vol. 34, No. 10, October 1979, 923-929.

46. Robinson et al., *Final Report on the 1982 Survey,* Chapter 7. Orend, *Socialization and Participation In The Arts.*

47. Lee Willerman, "Effects of Families on Intellectual Development."

48. Robinson et al., *Final Report on the 1982 Survey,* Chapter 7. Orend, *Socialization and Participation In The Arts.*

49. Susan G. Timmer, Jacquelynne Eccles, and Kerth O'Brien, "How Children Use Time;" and Martha S. Hill, "Patterns of Time Use," in F. Thomas Juster and Frank P. Stafford (Eds.), *Time, Goods, and Well-Being* (Ann Arbor, MI: Institute for Social Research, University of Michigan, 1985). John P. Robinson, *How Americans Use Time: A Social-Psychological Analysis of Everyday Behavior* (New York: Praeger, 1977).

50. Market Facts, Inc., *1983 Consumer Research Study,* 143-145.

51. Ibid., pp. 133-137.

52. Hill, "Patterns of Time Use," Table 7.1, 141.

53. William J. Bennett, *American Education: Making It Work* (Washington, DC: U.S. Government Printing Office, April 1988). Bloom, *Closing of the American Mind,* Cheney, *American Memory,* Hirsch, *Cultural Literacy.* Elizabeth Castor, "The Day of the Laureate: Warren Assumes His Mantle & Braves the Press, for Love of Poetry," *The Washington*

Post, October 7, 1986, Dl. Ravitch, Finn, *What Do Our 17-Year-Olds Know?;* The National Commission on Excellence in Education, A Nation at Risk: The Imperative for Educational Reform (Washington, DC: U.S. Government Printing Office, April 1983).

54. Bennett, *American Education,* 8-14. Congressional Budget Office, 1987, *Educational Achievement: Explanations and Implications of Recent Trends* (Washington, DC: Congressional Budget Office, 1987). Nicholas Zill and C.C. Rogers, "Recent Trends in the Well-Being of Children in the United States and their Implications for Public Policy," in Andrew Cherlin (Ed.), *Family Change and Public Policy* (Washington, DC: The Urban Institute Press, 1988), Chapter 2.

55. National Assessment of Educational Progress, *Literature and U.S. History.*

56. National Assessment of Educational Progress, *Reading, Thinking, and Writing: Results from the 1979-80 National Assessment of Reading and Literature* (Denver, CO: Education Commission of the States, October 1981).

57. National Assessment of Educational Progress, *Literacy: Profiles of America's Young Adults,* by Irwin S. Kirsch and Ann Jungeblut, Report No. 16-PL-02 (Princeton, NJ: Educational Testing Service, 1986).

58. National Assessment of Educational Progress, *The Reading Report Card, 1971-88: Trends from the Nation's Report Card,* by Ina V.S. Mullis and Lynn B. Jenkins, Report No. 19-R-01, (Princeton, NJ: Educational Testing Service, January 1990). Idem., *The Writing Report Card, 1984-88,* by Arthur N. Applebee, Judith A. Langer, Ina V.S. Mullis, and Lynn B. Jenkins, Report No. 19-W-01, (Princeton, NJ: Educational Testing Service, January 1990).

59. Alan C. Purves et al., *Reading and Literature: American Achievement in International Perspective,* NCTE Research Report No. 20 (Urbana, IL: National Council of Teachers of English, 1981).

60. Alan C. Purves, *Literature Education in Ten Countries,* International Association for the Evaluation of Educational Achievement, International Studies in Evaluation II (Stockholm: Almquist & Wiksell; New York: John Wiley, 1973).

61. College Board Admissions Testing Program, Statistical Summaries for Academic Years 1980-1981 through 1985-1986, unpublished tabulations supplied by Alicia Schmitt, Educational Testing Service, (Princeton, NJ, February 1987).

62. Yardley, "The Increasing Irrelevance of Writing."

63. Hilton Kramer, *The New Criterion Reader: The First Five Years* (New York: The Free Press, 1988). Jonathan Yardley, "Paradise Tossed: The Fall of Literary Standards," *The Washington Post,* January 11, 1988, B2.

64. Robert Pattison, *The Triumph of Vulgarity: Rock Music in the Mirror of Romanticism* (New York: Oxford University Press, 1987).

65. Rubenstein, E.A., G.A. Comstock, and J.P. Murray (Eds.), *Television and Social Behavior, (Vol. 4): Television in Day-to-Day Life: Patterns of Use,* (Washington, DC: US Government Printing Office, 1972). Schramm, Wilbur, *Big Media, Little Media: Tools and Technologies for Instruction,* (Beverly Hills, CA: Sage, 1977).

66. Heard, Alex, "Out There: Versed Things First," *The Washington Post Magazine,* April 17, 1988, 9-10.

67. Dan Lacy, "Publishing Enters the Eighties," in *The State of the Book World, 1980,* The Center for the Book Viewpoint Series, No. 4 (Washington, DC: The Library of Congress, 1980) 11-25; 23.

68. Market Facts, Inc., *1983 Consumer Research Study,* 133-136; 145.

69. Nicholas Spenceley, "The Readership of Literary Fiction: A Survey of Library Users in the Sheffield Area," M.A. Dissertation, Postgraduate School of Librarianship, Sheffield University, 1980. As described in Peter H. Mann, "The Novel in British Society."

70. Jonathan Yardley, "The Soft-Cover Salvation of Modern Fiction," *The Washington Post,* February 16, 1987, D2.

Index

Index